A SUBVERSIVE MOVEMENT

Martin Scott

Explorations in Theology

- volume three -

Boz Publications Ltd.

71-75 Shelton Street - Covent Garden - London - WC2H 9JQ - United Kingdom.

office@bozpublications.com / www.bozpublications.com

BOZ PUBLICATIONS

Copyright © 2021 Martin Scott

First published 2021 by Boz Publications Ltd

ISBN: 978-1-9164216-8-4

A CIP catalogue record for this book is available from the British Library.

Contents

PREFACE

YES, YOU MATTER

In the previous two volumes, I have tried to set out my convictions that the Gospel message was centred on God's vision for the world to be a place that reflected who he was; visibly displaying how to live in harmony with each other and creation. All relationships were to flow from a harmonious relationship to the God of creation. Inevitably this meant that the message (for example the message Paul carried) when presented within the context of a one-world dominating system was rightly heard to be deeply political, as it was a message, if followed, which would realign the world. At the centre of that message was a vision of a world that was aligned very differently to the world that the people in the first century were encountering; and not just for those people as the vision it proclaimed is equally different to our current world; indeed it contrasts every world that humanity has sought to shape since the 'fall'.

The 'political' message in no way diminishes the 'spiritual' message of being reconciled to God, and it certainly does not make that aspect unimportant. Indeed, quite to the contrary, for those who are reconciled to God are tasked with the responsibility of enabling others to find their place within this new potential order of life. The apostolic responsibility flows from a vision of this huge task, and the 'nobodies' who are called to be part of this governmental *ekklesia* are the movement through which God will accomplish his purposes.

This deeply spiritual element within the message, though, did not nullify the political element. The two elements sat together, with those who responded to the spiritual element of coming into relationship to the Creator God seeking to work with the Creator for the future of the world. That future world came into being through the resurrection of Jesus, and the disciples of Jesus knew that it would need his arrival to bring it in fully. They did not subscribe to the belief that if everyone simply tried harder then everything would change, and yet they also looked and worked for substantial changes that would mean the world in which they lived their lives would be more reflective, even if imperfectly so, of the age to come.

So what about 'me', for after all it is the nobodies who are the 'called'? When we write about a big apostolic vision and the scope of the Gospel being political, we can be in great danger of believing there is a misfit, as if God called the 'nobodies', but they, the nobodies, have to rise up so far beyond their abilities to complete the enormous task. Is it that the 'nobodies' have to become significant 'somebodies' for any level of real change to take place?

My conviction is that it is the multiplicity of the small (and the richness of diversity) that together, normally in an unplanned way, make the critical contribution to the further advance of this movement. The combination of small acts that are in alignment with heaven's direction and values are what make the difference. Not our big plans nor even our big visions! In the first volume, I had a chapter on the life of Judas who carried a major undisclosed weakness, and when that connected to his big vision, the combination became both his own downfall and the path to betraying Jesus. That combination needs to remain as a salutary lesson to us all. Our big vision might not simply be our downfall but could become the setback to the very kingdom that we desire to come. Whereas our humble acts surely fit the description that Jesus gave concerning the 'cup of cold water' given in his name.

There has been a wonderful re-discovery in many evangelical and charismatic circles of the pull to engage with the world. I have observed how there has been a healthy move forward from emphasising prayer to change the spiritual environment; likewise, it appears that many who have been impacted by refreshing Spiritual awakenings are increasingly asking, 'and where is all this going?'[1] That can only be healthy as (assuming there has been a real shift) Jesus said that if we cast out a 'demon' but do not deal with the space that was inhabited by that demon the latter state can be much worse than the former. His application of that was not to an individual who had found freedom, but to a generation's experience.[2] It was certainly proved true concerning the generation that did not receive his presence and message.

Ephesus

In Ephesus (Acts 19), there is a wonderful record of the impact of the Pauline Gospel. We read of 'salvations', the renouncing of occult practices with the burning of literature, and we read of miracles and healings. There seems to be a territorial aspect to this impact as the Pauline message was heard by all, Jew and Greek, throughout the province of Asia (Acts 19:10).

The territory that is named is the territory over which Artemis of the Ephesians supposedly reigned and was worshipped. Not surprisingly the objection to Paul, his activities and message, centred in on accusations that he had blasphemed against the goddess Artemis. There was a perception that her status was under huge threat.

1: In the above there is no negativity concerning the prayer nor the Spiritual (capitalised as I attribute this to the Spirit) awakenings. My suggestion is that those are foundations for the body of Christ to be repositioned in and engaged with the world.

2 'That is how it will be with this wicked generation' (Matt. 12:45).

Indeed that threat was a very real threat, and I consider that when there is a real shift with respect to the spiritual powers there will also be a manifestation in the economic realm. For this reason, it is not surprising that this was the focus of the riot. A backlash that wants to protect the economy should not surprise us as Jesus positioned allegiance to God and to Mammon at opposite ends of the spectrum; and the final book, Revelation, has much to say about economics and that those who follow the Lamb will find that there are restrictions placed on them in order to prevent them 'buying and selling'.[3]

Seven Mountains of Influence

The Gospel impact was not simply a private one, with individual lives being changed, but a corporate one that affected the whole life of the city. Hence any attention that is turned to 'what does the Gospel mean for society and how can we engage?' can only be very healthy.

[T]here is not a square inch in the whole domain of our human existence over which Christ, who is Sovereign over all, does not cry: 'Mine!'

(the former Prime Minister of the Netherlands and neo-Calvinist, Abraham Kuyper 1837-1920)

Jesus is indeed Lord of all, but it is the outworking of statements, such as the one Kuyper made, that remains the challenge. Creation came into being through Christ, and his redemptive death is for the future of creation; hence the cry of 'Mine' is legitimate. 'Jesus is Lord' is a public statement, but how do we live out that conviction? Kuyper himself gave space to those of all faiths, so perhaps he sought to apply the statement generously. His premise has certainly resonated with

---

3 For this reason I do not consider the most pressing issue for the believer is how to avoid an 'electronic chip' or something similar, but to discover the reality of an economy that is based on gift. Paul wrote about the matter of 'giving and receiving' (Phil. 4:15). That is the foundation for a radical economy and one that is counter to the 'buying and selling' economy.

many and in recent years has been made popular under an umbrella of 'the seven mountains of influence'[4] that shape public life, with which those who follow Christ need to engage.

Thus far so good! As always, it is the application of our beliefs that is so important. Add to Kuyper's statement that the claims of Christ reach into the public sphere, a practical understanding that statistically the top 3% within the various spheres are the ones who ultimately bring about the influence, and it is quick to see where this can lead.

The Gospel is not a private message, but a public declaration that Jesus is Lord of all; the *ekklesia* of God is the intended catalyst through which transformation comes; we pray and work for the kingdom to come, the will of God on earth as in heaven... and I understand that if we combine those truths with such teaching as 'the seven mountains of influence' that a practical process can be set in motion.

With this emphasis, at best, we have some practical understanding and subsequent training can be implemented to show how, as believers, we can be involved wherever we find ourselves positioned to contribute positively in bringing about healthy change. However, at worst, the vision can become a paradigm that fosters the imposing of our 'values' on the world, with the goal of becoming part of the influential minority who can legislate change from the top down. Such an approach is nothing better than a Christianised version of 'sharia'[5] law, and a reverting back to Christendom that fuelled such atrocities as the Crusades. The result of such an extreme approach

---

4 These are normally enumerated as: religion, family, education, government, media, arts & entertainment, business.

5 Religious law forming part of the Islamic tradition. I argue that it is not too different in concept from those who wish for a Christian nation with supposed biblical standards legislated for.

can only be that of yet another round of religious wars.[6]

Language carries meaning, and it is very difficult to find the language that best describes a concept. Even a word such as 'parent', 'mother', or 'father' might arguably have an inherent meaning but what the word means to someone (how it is heard and what reaction results) is shaped by the person's own perception mainly developed because of their history.

One could argue that the language of 'seven mountains of influence' is simply language, but combine the language of 'mountains' with the suggestion that the 'top' 3% are the shapers, and it is very hard to understand it as *simply* language. The language suggests a world-view that change takes place from the top-down, that importance is attached to being at the top, and that the exercise of power is one that ultimately imposes our vision of God's government on others.

I suspect there is a deep belief among many who profess the Christian faith that 'sovereignty', in the sense of imposing a rule, is indeed the way God governs. To hold to that view, any *kenosis* (self-emptying on behalf of others) that was manifested in the incarnation does not become a revelation of who God is, but simply a temporary posture. I hold that in the outpoured servant-giving life of Jesus we indeed see who God is, that the weakness and shame of the cross is truly where the glory of God is revealed to us.

Jesus, with a towel around his waist, washing the disciples' feet is one of those images that has left a sacred mark on our world. In John Chapter 1, he had come to his own (both in terms of his 'own people' and to that which was his own, the wider creation) but had been rejected; later, though in the same Gospel (chapter 13), he sat down with 'his own', those who had received him, those to whom he

---

6 And when there is a 'religious' mountain that Christianity is supposed to shape it is very hard to see how a religious war is not the result. Ironically the founder of the Christian faith came to bring the mountains down!

had revealed the Father. That act of washing feet was deeply revealing of who the Father was. Not a sovereign who gets offended, but one who takes on the task that was beneath almost one and all, for no Hebrew slave could be enforced to wash feet.

Kings and Priests

Using simpler language than that of 'seven mountains' is the language of 'kings and priests'. The term 'kings' being used to describe the call of those who are believers involved in the marketplace, and 'priests' for those whose work and focus is within the church. Again, no one deserves to be disagreed with simply based on the language being used, so I wish to tread carefully, as we all struggle to find appropriate language. I appreciate the positive aspect of trying to find ways of valuing those who are engaged in the important area of the marketplace, engaging with the world, and in using the term 'kings' for those who are working where we all want to see a tangible expression of the kingdom of God be expressed. If 'king' means servants who seek to lovingly be agents of the kingdom this term might have some traction but the word 'king' comes with too many connotations of 'above' and 'ruling' to be possible to redeem.

So in treading carefully, I still have to say, 'However!' The division of 'kings' and 'priests' is a rather crude way of understanding the phrase that has been influential in these writings, the 'kingdom of priests' terminology. The kingdom that is described though is not made up of the two divisions that are implied by the language of 'kings and priests', but is a kingdom that consists of priests, and in such a kingdom there are no 'kings'.

There are those who are called to work within the body but (apologies to those of the more sacramental approach) the term 'priest' does not seem appropriate. The priesthood that we encounter from Exodus 19 onwards is a corporate priesthood consisting of the whole body of people. It is a description of believers whose task is to stand representatively for the world, between what is and what is to come. The most common term in the NT for those who work and derive income from 'church work' is that they 'live by the gospel', and an often used term, 'living by faith', is not something that should be used exclusively for such people as all believers are required to live by faith, and that is not faith in the pay packet at the end of the month!

A different flow than power

I trust I have not been too harsh in pushing back against the language that is used to help reposition the body of Christ. I know many who use the kind of language I have described and exhibit more of the servant nature of the Trinity than I do, so I wish again to affirm the real issue is not language but the outworking. Language, though, can shape practice, and it is for that reason I think it is important. Any language that lends itself to the suggestion that we should aim to be 'over' and to 'rule' has to be questioned. We do not have authority over people; true life flows where there is a mutual submission one to another, and any authority we have 'over' is to be over the works of the devil.

The terms 'seven mountains of influence' or 'kings and priests' do not intrinsically critique the root issue of power, and how 'rulership' is not through the giving of commands but through loving, laid-down service. There are some very revealing Scriptures on the way a God-movement impacts the wider world. One I find hard to memorise but reveals so much amidst a set of names, is Luke 3:1-3.

In the fifteenth year of the reign of Tiberius Caesar
- when Pontius Pilate was governor of Judea, Herod
tetrarch of Galilee, his brother Philip tetrarch of Iturea
and Traconitis, and Lysanias tetrarch of Abilene -
during the high-priesthood of Annas and Caiaphas,
the word of God came to John son of
Zechariah in the wilderness.

Caesar is on the throne, far away from life in Israel, but all his sub-rulers are much closer to hand, and to complicate things even a little more, the joint high-priesthood continues to allow the religious life to be subjugated to Rome. The whole situation is locked up, a situation that was indeed a challenge to any concept of the public sphere changing! Too often in our situation, a context that is seldom even close to paralleling such an all-but-one-world government, we have assumed that change will take place when 'God's appointed person' is in power, when legislation that is 'biblical' can be set in place through government. I passionately believe that God is deeply interested in the government that is in place, but before we explore such beliefs we need to ensure that we have heard the statement that 'the word of God came to John son of Zechariah in the wilderness'.

God does not move to replace the current Caesar, nor the various kings, nor does he even install a high-priest chosen from the 'evangelical God-fearing' camp. That alone should be a sobering perspective to hold us back from finding the 'Christian' or 'Christian-friendly' one for the position of power.

Given that we are living between the 'already' and the 'not-yet' any engagement with power will be messy. Messy as we engage, and also messy among ourselves as we seek the best path forward. We can read the same Bible but come to vastly different conclusions. That can be a challenge that divides or an enriching process. What proves to be unhelpful is a dogmatism that proclaims that we have the one and only path!

A movement that began in the desert, the place abandoned by God, the supposed stronghold of the demonic, but calling to memory the journey of departure from Egypt. Egypt, the place that supplied all that was needed, but at a price - the place that established the norms. In this new movement that was going to challenge the legitimacy of Caesar's rule, God's word first came in the place that symbolised departure, in the place where the original journey began, where they were called to be a kingdom of priests. Likewise, if we are going to be those who make a difference, there has to be the weaning from the dependency on the established powers.

In 2005 just after Bush had been elected as president, I was in the USA in the early months of that year. Reading, as I was at the time, through Luke's Gospel and the book of Revelation, something came to me strongly about the future of the political scene in that land. I said that in 2008 the elected candidate would not be the one that they (white, middle-class, charismatic Christians) would have desired. But if they could not embrace that person in 08 that a 'double-blow' would come their way in 2012. In the years that followed, I listened to many rumours about the subsequent president-elect, Barack Obama. One such rumour, in the run-up to the 08 election, I heard from a youth pastor addressing young people. He was calling for a vote for the candidate running against Obama, proclaiming that Obama was a 'Muslim'. I challenged him after the gathering with, 'there is no evidence that he is a Muslim; indeed everything points to him having faith in Jesus.' His reply was, 'I know, but it helps our cause to say he is a Muslim.' I had never come across anything so blatant before.

Back to what I said; 2012 would be a double blow but that God would use it to help them see that they were already deceived. The aspect of deception that makes it very hard to discern is that it does not occur when we think we are deceived. If I am driving to a destination but inadvertently make a wrong turn, it is only when I pass some landscape that should not be present on the journey that I realise I have made a mistake, the mistake having taken place sometime earlier. The realisation that I am not on the right road alerts me that I have been deceived, and the deception took place prior to that realisation. I suggested that the deception was related to the belief that, 'if we get the right person in the White House, then things will change'. The deception was in the alignment to power. That story might be set in a north American situation, but it can be replicated throughout the world. It might be a story about major power at the top, but we could substitute it for all sorts of power at a lower level.

I appreciate that I write as one deeply influenced by the Anabaptist view of church and state, with the conviction that there is no such thing as a 'Christian' country. Even without that influence, it is very difficult to abstract the idea of a 'Christian' nation. It seems to me we are dealing with terminology that does not mix.[7] By definition, the Christian 'population' is not bounded by borders and walls; it does not defend itself through military means, nor seek to protect its own self-interests. The concept of 'Christian nation' is absent from Scripture, with the corporate scattered people of God both being aliens within the world while identifying themselves as being a holy nation.

There is one final concept that feeds into the 'Christian nation' perspective, using Matthew 25:31-46 to suggest that there are/will be 'sheep' and 'goat' nations. The text unfolds with a picture of judgement (perhaps final judgement, but more likely a reflection of the days following the Jewish Wars of 66-70AD). The peoples (the nations, another word also for the Gentiles) are gathered and they are separated as to how they historically treated those who were in trouble. Some who would have self-designated themselves as righteous will not receive a reward, and some who acted with generosity will receive a reward, even though they were unaware of the eternal value of what they were doing. The concept of there being whole nations that can be categorised as 'sheep' or others labelled as 'goat' nations seems totally absent.

---

7 Israel was to be a theocracy, but failed many times over. Even if we were to suggest Israel was the model, there is a very big difference from the 'nations' of Scripture and the 'nation-state' of today.

The Jesus Movement

The movement that began in the wilderness took Jesus to Jerusalem, the centre of religion. At the centre of his mission was the undoing of religion; religion that left God inaccessible and distant. If there is a false tie between religion and power, God will remain distant to us, and there will be no effective advance. Religion, in whatever form, has to be broken so that life can be experienced.

The death of Jesus is multi-faceted, but religion, in all its forms, was nailed to the cross. The death in Jerusalem, significantly described as an 'exodus',[8] was precisely that. The former Exodus took place in Egypt to set the people free to go to the Promised Land; this 'Jesus' Exodus' was going to take place in Jerusalem, now the place of bondage under Roman imperial rule, and the place that kept captive the people of God from their destiny. An Exodus from Egypt to go on a journey to the Promised Land was the former experience; after the cross they would be released from their captivity to journey to the promised lands, this Paul characteristically captures in Romans 4:13 by saying that Abraham was not promised a land but that he would inherit the world! Something of a shift takes place when we read the Old Testament through the eyes of a Jew such as Paul.

The Exodus in Jerusalem broke the captivity of the centre and from there the path to Rome, the place that was the centre of the world, was opened. From the wilderness with John to climactic days in Jerusalem with Jesus, and on to Rome with Paul. Once we move beyond a religious framework to a Gospel framework, we too can participate in Paul's journey to the world.

In writing this volume, I have the expectation that it will provoke the greatest disagreement, for it is at this point when we are looking at

---

8 Luke 9:3, translated as 'departure' but the normal word for the Exodus is used. Theological-ly, as I suggest above, this is heavy with meaning.

how we engage with the world that the greatest differences will show up in our approaches. We will outwork our involvement with the world differently but from our own place of conviction.

Regardless of how we express this outworking for the Gospel, we have to do so from a heart of love, being willing servants and not self-promoting. Maybe one other aspect is necessary, that we do so with a deep genuineness.

There was an era when shops and supermarkets did not open on a Sunday in the UK. The debate concerning making a change to the legislation was intense, and there was at the time a Christian campaign entitled 'Keep Sunday Special'. It argued its case mainly on the basis that it was healthy that people could have some time away from work; a break was good, and there would be a detrimental effect on family life if Sunday trading was allowed. I remember the (slightly tongue-in-cheek) campaign of a friend to pull Christians behind a 'Keep Wednesday Special' campaign that would tick all the same boxes. Family life, healthy rest rhythms would be ensured by doing so. His campaign did not prosper!

The 'Wednesday' campaign was motivated to provoke a level of honesty. Were the arguments being advanced, the real arguments, or was the 'Keep Sunday Special' campaign really centred on making sure that Sunday (church) life was not going to be disturbed?

I appreciate that we need wisdom in how we make our arguments heard, with the language chosen being important, but if we do not really believe in the arguments we are advancing and only use them because they might get our wishes fulfilled - then I object to that. The 'Keep Sunday Special' campaign failed, and I find it revealing that once the law was passed how many believers were among those who were glad for Sunday opening? I do not know of any who campaigned who have since avoided entering a store on a Sunday!

We are not in this life to promote our way or a way of life that enhances us. Our service is for those beyond us, and this will totally shape our approach.

CHAPTER 1

AESTHETICALLY GOOD

*The Lord God made all kinds of trees grow out
of the ground - trees that were pleasing to
the eye and good for food.*

- *(Gen. 2:9)* **-**

Creation, even imperfect creation, speaks loudly, and this verse in the early chapters of our sacred volume is so insightful. Creation was proclaimed good (not perfect, as good indicates a start, not an end) and the trees are commented on as being good at two levels. The functional one of providing food and at the aesthetic level of being pleasing to the eye. The verses preceding the one I quoted tells us that humanity was created to work the ground in response to the rain from heaven. It is not a stretch at all to suggest therefore that working with creation was intended to be for functional and aesthetic purposes.

Art is not an add on to human life, though sadly in some settings that are focused on simply surviving, it can easily be labelled as a luxury. That is not a comment on art but on how far we have allowed life to descend below the human level.

God is creative, and if humanity is created to image him, there should be a lively expression of creativity in society. Like so much of life, gifts from heaven have been commodified. Art is bought as an investment, and some artists prosper, while many cannot make a living from their gift to humanity. The attraction of the talent-shows, that profile unknown amateur talent, is that we are all blown away by the extraordinary gifts that are among us. And of course, for every previously unbeknown talent that is discovered on those shows we will never know how many will remain undiscovered.

The word 'amateur' is interesting as it comes from the Latin 'amo', meaning 'I love'. It has often come to mean 'second rate', but really should mark all those who are involved in the arts. A love for colour, sound and creativity, with two eyes focused on producing something that is pleasant to see, hear, or be impacted by, and without a focus on the supposed bottom line. Earning money is a necessity, but when it completely dictates the boundaries of what art becomes visible, we have yet again a sad commentary on our world.

Let me convince you

If words, written and spoken, are one's trade we love to argue, to dispute, to put up straw targets just to knock them down! We want to convince people of how right we are (sub-text: how wrong they are). The discussion is at a mind-to-mind, concept-to-concept level. Occasionally we win. The win, though, is normally at a head level, which can be valuable, but simply winning an argument does not often shift something at a heart level.

The intellect is to be honoured, and there are causes that need to be won in the public arena at an intellectual level, but there is another level to our personal and corporate psyche that sits deeper than the intellect. Win the 'argument' there, and the intellect will have to catch up. I am speaking of the imagination.

The imagination has been downgraded in many circles, and certainly in many Protestant oriented circles, where all images were removed from the architecture. I understand the reason for that (supposed idolatry), but there has probably been a loss in the midst of the reaction. In many Christian circles, there has been a re-focus on the arts with an emphasis on such things as sacred dance or professional Christian music. That can be welcomed, but when we understand the purpose of the *ekklesia* is to care for, take responsibility for and to healthily shape the world in a justice direction, there also has to be music, dance and art that does not have a label on it stamping it as 'Christian', but that comes out of the heart of those shaped by the Jesus narrative.

For that to carry weight, we need ever so many amateurs in love with the Author of creativity and their own creative craft. Such people energised by the Spirit are vital to touch the imagination. If we are ever going to pull the world to a different future, it will only happen when there is the experience of seeing through different eyes. The power of Martin Luther King's speech was in the words, 'I have a dream'. He expressed his sight of a different world.

The book of Scripture I like the best is the final one. I am glad that nowhere are we told to understand it as a whole, and that those who read it, who hear it, are those who are blessed. I sometimes wish I could hear it the same way as the first audience heard it. I find it hard to use words that convey the kind of book it is, but it is certainly a book full of images. It contains many words, but the effect of hearing those words would be as if one were exposed to what would seem as never-ending film clips, protest art, political cartoons, emotive music and other disturbing elements. The end result for those original hearers would have been a total disorientation.

We need a huge disorientation. Phrases such as 'money makes the world go round' are phrases that describe a supposed normalised orientation. The phrase becomes the reality, and nothing can be imagined outside of that normality. Art, art and yet more art is what is necessary to break those cycles. Yes, there are arguments to be won, there are new concepts to be explained, but there must also be huge incisions brought to society's norms that will allow space for the alternative.

I appreciate that I am strongly suggesting that the creative arts are to be disruptive, but I have done that to make a point. Not all art is there to disrupt, but all art should touch us at a level deeper than the conceptual. It is to help us 'feel', and therefore art will certainly not always be 'nice'.

Disruptive, but not simply destructive. The Gospel comes to disrupt, but always to open up doors to a future. There is always hope even in the context of a wake-up call that sobers. Not every piece of art can carry a full message, but amidst the critique of what is considered 'normal' some insight into a different world should be opened.

What is termed worship music can be helpful in putting us in touch with God, but can also be unhelpful if it puts us out of touch with the world. The Psalms, which are often described as the hymn book of the Jewish world, mention God over and over, but we also find there the songs of lament about the state of the world, and enough protest songs to confront all manner of injustices. We might need more songs that proclaim 'God is great', but we certainly need a flood of songs that will proclaim 'We don't need a Christian president', and those songs will probably have a few expletives thrown in.

Fashion - the place to work

I have never had on my résumé the words 'fashion guru', so like many things I write about, I write about them. I had a young lady come to me many years ago, asking if I would pray for her regarding her work. I said I would love to and asked what work she was involved in. She replied, 'I am a fashion designer.' I instantly responded that I would love to pray for her and that her career was exactly where Christians should be involved and went on to suggest that anyone who had a belief in the resurrection of the dead had something to bring to the world of fashion that others did not. A believer and the fashion industry, made for one another.[1]

Before I continue the story, let me digress just for a moment. Many Christians who repeat the creed concerning the resurrection of the dead, probably do not believe in the resurrection of the dead. They tend to reduce it to mean something like 'life after death'. The Jewish hope was not that real life begins after death, once we escape this world, but that real, God-filled life is to be experienced here in bodily form. Such a belief necessitated the conviction that those who had died and were righteous would be raised from the dead to participate in life here in bodily form. To simply believe in life after death was something that was very common in Greek circles; not Jewish, nor early Christian circles.

Physical, bodily life is so strong in Scripture, and one could suggest that there is no greater affirmation for non-ending bodily existence than the resurrection cry that, 'He is not here, He is risen.'

Back to the story; I quickly jumped to 2 Corinthians 5 to explain that Paul had a nervousness about life after death. His nervousness was focused on his desire not to appear naked, and by that he meant bodiless. It seems unclear what the Bible teaches about life after death, but there just might be an interim period of bodiless existence. This seems to be what Paul is reflecting on, and it was this that he called 'nakedness' when he would somehow be less than he was.

---

1 So much of the fashion industry, particularly the high end, carries a 'snob' element within it. That aspect, which so often covers over a person's real identity, means that, as in most industries, there are also great challenges for a believer and their involvement in the fashion world. I also acknowledge that many people in our world have no choice over their clothing. The story I am telling has a narrow application and addressed to those who have choice.

Clothes are not simply intended to cover modesty, nor simply to keep us warm, but to enable us to express ourselves, our innerness to be expressed in an external way. Often clothing shows off and exploits a sexuality that simply objectifies the person, so I went on to explain that a believer who understood that fashion is to enable someone to express their core being is in the right industry. I said that models should be asking if 'so and so is exhibiting?', and if the reply was in the affirmative, they should then be asking if they could wear those clothes, as when they wear them they feel clean, and that they never feel more themselves, nor more positively about themselves than when they wear those clothes.

Far-fetched? No, I do not think so. The fashion industry has often been exploitative, with the word 'sexy' simply meaning sexualised. The two words in reality, are poles apart.

Good to look at. It felt good. Art.

And 'I felt so disoriented'; 'I was disturbed'. Art.

Many tribal situations understand the value of the liminal space. In those contexts as a young person reached the point of leaving childhood to enter adulthood often the ritual involved disorientation, of taking the person to a space at the edge of their world where there could be no reverting back to previous norms. The experience is often traumatic, but is based on an understanding that a major transition such as moving into adulthood is not engaged in as a gentle process.

Disorientation and liminality are so often needed to help catalyse change. At first the experience might be too shocking to benefit from, but later the value can be understood. We need the artists. Christian artists. Artists who have been energised by the Spirit. Maybe not so many will become professional, but they can all be amateurs.

It is time to awaken the imagination if we want a different future.

CHAPTER 2

A NECESSARY CHAPTER

A chapter on the arts was a nice gentle way to highlight how any communication needs more than words to bring about change. In that chapter I said that art has often been commodified, becoming the collector's piece, sometimes because of a deep appreciation of the art but often because of the perceived investment value. One piece bought for monetary reasons while other artists, who put their heart and soul into something (not to mention many hours), cannot make a living from their gift to society. It leads me to this chapter, a necessary one, on money, work and value.

The archaeologists report that between the 10th and the 8th century BC there were many economic changes in the land of Israel. Over those two centuries, a huge discrepancy grows between the size of houses. (Maybe relevant, the 10th Century is the beginning of the monarchical period; the appointment of a king 'so that we might be like the nations' maybe also increased the economic divides.) We might take the view that the prosperity that abounded (for some) was evidence as to how God had blessed, but the 8th-century prophets viewed it very differently. This is the rise of the critical voices of the prophets who connected social inequality to a faithlessness to the covenant. There is a poignant example in Amos 4:1-4,

Hear this word,
you cows of Bashan on Mount Samaria,
you women who oppress the poor and crush the needy
and say to your husbands, "Bring us some drinks!"
The Sovereign Lord has sworn by his holiness:
"The time will surely come when you will be
taken away with hooks, the last of you with fishhooks.
You will each go straight out through breaches in
the wall, and you will be cast out toward Harmon,"
declares the Lord. Go to Bethel and sin;
go to Gilgal and sin yet more.
Bring your sacrifices every morning,
your tithes every three years.

Continuing to tithe and sacrifice in the appointed way was exposed as a farce as there was no justice, no semblance of an egalitarian society. In the life of Israel, the law stipulated an intentional levelling through the system of Sabbath, the seventh year Sabbath and a radical Jubilee every fiftieth year when there was a reboot to the whole of society.

Before wading in to some of these major issues a gentle proviso that I will try and pick up in a later chapter. The gentle proviso is, 'but we have to be practical.' Agreed! We are not looking for something that is perfect for we wait for the day 'when the perfect comes'; we live in a fallen world, and in that world we have to learn how to compromise. The compromises that we are to be involved in though are to be redemptive. Redemption does not bring us to perfection in the immediate but re-aligns us so that there is a before and an after, so that we are not left the same, and the after is better than the before. Jesus quoted the Scripture that 'the poor you will have with you always' (John 12:8 quoting Deut. 15:11), and that surely is true. However, we cannot use it as if Jesus intended us to be unmoved or inactive about inequalities. The Scripture that Jesus quoted, Deut. 15:11 says:

There will always be poor people in the land.
Therefore I command you to be openhanded
toward your fellow Israelites who are poor
and needy in your land.

There is a reality that there will always be those who experience poverty, and in the light of that there has to be a spirit of generosity, for such was the commandment God gave them. The wider passage exhorts us to be generous, to cancel debts, to help liberate and to truly work toward the goal of eradicating poverty.

The wider context does not allow us to passively accept issues of poverty, but we still have the situation that Jesus received the over-the-top lavish gift (waste?) of the perfume that anointed him for the future. Jesus was able to relate to those who were wealthy and those who were not; he did not primarily see people through their financial standing but as people with value. He did not carry a poverty mentality and could receive the luxury of the gift. In this situation he received what was given, and saw beyond the gift to the love expressed by the giver; I suggest his focus was on the person not on the value of the gift. Meanwhile, Judas (and many of us?) saw the value of the gift and missed the significance of what was taking place and the love being expressed.

The Gospel sets out the eschatological focus and then deals with the present in both real and redemptive terms. It does not call us to live with a utopian vision, nor does it allow us to be passive. The *ekklesia* is present in the world to bring about change, and we are in a world that is all but a runaway train hellbent on destruction. The original sin of consumerism, of moving boundaries for personal gain has to be addressed. This chapter is focused on money (or maybe better put as Mammon), but it could equally address the ecological crisis which is yet another sign that we have, as a race, been consistently moving boundary markers for personal gain.

What is work?

In the COVID-19 lockdown during the time that I am writing these volumes, an interesting phrase has developed. It is the phrase 'essential workers'. Suddenly those who were formerly invisible have become visible. Care professions, street cleaners, vegetable growers, emergency service workers and the like have all been awarded the title. Many of those whose salaries have been among the lowest in society have been applauded. Meanwhile, no-one has written about the hedge fund managers, or international finance traders as being part of the elite group of 'essential workers'! There has been, at least at a verbal level, a re-assessment of how work is defined. I am not suggesting that those involved in the financial sector are not working, simply that in times of crises a healthy re-assessment takes place; perhaps indicating that once such crises have been overcome the re-assessment should remain.

Inhabiting, as we do, a fallen world, there are many careers that are present that will not continue in the age to come, and most of those are in the economic realm. We could be intensely critical and write off all such workers, but we have to grapple with the world as we find it, and money is intensely complex, both illustrating the creativity of humanity,[1] and the inevitable effect it has on the increasing gap between those who have much more than enough and those who are below the poverty level.

Money and economic theory are complex, but having said that we also need to be clear. There are 'careers' that are off bounds for a follower of Jesus. For example, I do not expect that anyone suggests

---

1 In a very real sense 'money' does not exist. It has increasingly moved away from representing something tangible, to being figures on a computer screen. Crazily, or creatively, the more debt, the more money that can be created! When we read that the stock market has 'lost' x billion it is not a measure of how much money was there previously, but in reality, a reference to the loss of confidence. If I lose some money and someone else finds it, the money simply circulates, but the 'loss' the stock market suffers cannot be found by someone else. The 'money' has disappeared, thus indicating it was never a tangible substance. Creativity from almost nothing could be applauded, or critiqued.

that a believer could own a company that sold people into the slave trade. I suspect too that we would draw a line at owning a chain of gambling shops - although I have met a number of believers, including pastors, who were more than happy to engage with the various tables in those settings. There are careers and jobs that do a certain amount of damage, and those are the ones that we have to be careful about engaging with, and yet our fallen environment means we cannot always be perfect! A rule of thumb should be that we are always looking to be redemptive and that the accepted bottom line of 'profit' should not be the deciding factor; the bottom line of enhancing the lives of 'people' has to be the major directive.

The growing emphasis among believers that there is no such thing as a 'secular' job, with work being sacred, has to be welcomed. However, that emphasis has often only been applied to those in the work-place who earn more money, with them being the ones that are given the higher profile. Sometimes one could be forgiven for thinking the only issue was helping such people understand that they could be greater givers to the cause of the kingdom, with no question as to how the money was obtained. If I were to become a very efficient bank robber, I too could become a greater giver! If that were to happen, I hope someone would ask the hard question and bring about a correction and not simply rejoice over my 'tithe'. How the money was sourced would be an important part of the equation.

Ladies and gentlemen, the kingdom is radical. Hard questions are asked, and have to be, as transforming a corrupt, oppressive system is what is required.

If one of the signs that we are headed in the right direction is that we will not be allowed to buy and to sell, we cannot simply evaluate kingdom success on the basis of money being earned. Indeed a kingdom value (maybe) should be based on money not being earned!

This whole area is messy. I do not come to it with the answers, but I take heart that if it is messy, I probably can't mess it up any more than it already is. If I provoke a reaction that is good, and then if we all seek to respond tentatively with our own revelation, perhaps we could imperfectly pull our world in a redemptive direction.

Work and creation

In the early chapters of Genesis, there are some important revelations that are given to us about God. One revelation is that he is a worker, and on the seventh day, he rested from his work. Humanity, made in the image of God, was to continue that work, perhaps even to bring it to completion. I don't think it pushes the narrative too far to suggest that the direction for the work was to bring all of creation to its fullness, from a 'good' beginning to a fitting and glorious completion. The original garden was marked as a defined area where something could begin, and one supposes that the boundaries would have been pushed back until through the work of humanity 'the whole earth would have been filled with the glory of God as the waters cover the seas.'

We see in the garden the generosity and provision of God along with time for reflection. That was the context for those primordial humans to look after the land. Regardless, whether there was a historic fall or not, we read of the opposition expressed within the land to produce. Far from being a land flowing with milk and honey we read of thorns and thistles, and so there would be considerable effort required for the land to yield good fruit. Work becomes hard, it would result in sweat, yet in spite of the resistance there was the promise of a profitable outcome.

If we continue to read the Old Testament we find that entrepreneurship is seen as a gift from God, but that there are limitations placed on how that gift is developed and expressed. Exploitation of others, seen in the continual warning not to move boundary markers, and the maximisation of profits, witnessed by the command not to harvest to the edge of the field, were forbidden. (We can add the very important principle of the reset with Jubilee and we can understand that rampant perpetual growth was strongly legislated against.)

Work, as portrayed in those early chapters of Genesis, relates to how this current world is stewarded, and as we read further, the concept of exploitation, even when exercised through an entrepreneurial gift, was seen as illegitimate. Such exploitative activity, even if it pulled in huge sums of money, would not be classed as 'work'.

This disconnection of money from work is an important element. Those who labour are worthy of a reward, but not every act of obtaining finances can be claimed to stem from work. This should not be a surprise as even the devil offered Jesus a great reward in the wilderness, offering him the wealth of the nations. A person might put in many hours, they might apply themselves and exercise their gifts, and through that activity produce enormous sums of money that some others might also benefit from, but how the activity relates to creation would be an important factor for the Bible to describe the activity as 'work'.

In 2 Thessalonians 3:10, Paul says that the person who 'is unwilling to work shall not eat'. This is not some hard-line approach he advocated where he would have wanted legislation that did not provide for those who were unemployed. The text runs deep, and I believe again calls us to redefine the very word 'work'. He did not say if a person does not earn money, they should not eat. That is to give to Paul our world-view of the term unemployed, where in our world the word effectively means 'not working'. To be unemployed might mean we do not take home a paycheck at the end of the week, but to be unemployed does not necessarily mean that the person is not working; work being shaped by the stewardship of the wider world of creation and people. Indeed we could also add that the person who is putting in many hours and bringing home a sum of money might not be working! Now applying Paul's suggestion would indeed be a very radical piece of legislation.

We have complicated things enormously through what has developed. We have those who can earn money, and huge sums of money, through simply using the money they already have. Investing in shares so that a company is beholden to them was not something that was envisaged in the Bible, and can work against the enhancement of creation.

And then we have money itself, or money in its current form, where the largest proportion of it simply does not exist. When we read that the stock market has had x billions wiped off its value, it should also raise for us a question as to the 'reality' of what we call money.

Money in our world has become a set of numbers that is literally created on the basis of debt. At a very real level, the more debt, the more money! If we were to try at a personal level to run our finances on the same basis as nations and national banks do, we would soon find ourselves in court, as we would rightly be on trial for being at the centre of a huge financial scam.

In the previous paragraphs, it might appear that I have sought to demonise how the relationship between work and finances has evolved, so I need to redress that perspective some. The development of money can be seen as huge creativity, even a measure of creation ex-nihilo(!) that humanity has pulled out of the bag, and to enable money to make money could be admired. I do not deny that, but I consider that we also need to seek to hold such creativity in check; otherwise, we will simply produce another tower of Babel, where the flow of society was to build a tower that reached to heaven, and the people could make a name for themselves. The Genesis text that recounts the tower of Babel incident has a deep irony within it - the tower was going to reach heaven, but in reality was so miniscule that God 'came down' to see it! We have to imbibe a God-perspective to counteract how easily we can be impressed by something so insignificant, by that which contains little real value.

The rampant, unchecked capitalism, epitomised in the neo-liberal approach can never be justified. Profit as the bottom line and a belief in the necessity of a certain level of unemployment simply does not line up with the generosity of God. A belief in the 'invisible hand of the market' as the great regulator is surely an a-Theism that bows at the feet of an idol. That kind of capitalism strongly lines up at significant points with the demonising work that dehumanises.

Engaging with the world that we inhabit is such a challenge. We might be tempted to opt-out by adopting an alternative lifestyle. Such an approach can be challenged as simply to drop out, to no longer make a contribution, but there might be an element of that approach that is embodying a prophetic oppositional stance to the runaway world where finance and its institutions, rules.[2] Conversely, we might view the issues as so complex that we do not even begin to critique what we see around us, perhaps hoping that if we profit from it and are generous then perhaps the whole scene will be baptised.

Our relation to money is complex, but there is a simple thread that has to run through our response, that thread being we cannot afford to serve Mammon.

Work - new creation

We work now for the future. What we are involved in should be storing up treasure. In a later volume, I will seek to outline my considerations on eschatology where we cannot build the kingdom, but that we are producing the building blocks that will build the kingdom (the 'New Jerusalem' that John saw). With this concept, work has an eternal value. What we do, and maybe more importantly,

---

2 The critique that those who opt out do not pay into the system (tax, national insurance etc.) but seek to use the system when it is to their convenience (health care, for example) seems very valid. Taxation being a part of the Old Testament set-up, where tithing was not simply for the support of a priesthood, but for the marginalised as well (there were three 'tithes': a Levitical one, a festival tithe and a poor tithe). Given the different tithe instructions the final proportion was not 1/10 of one's income but perhaps even as high as 23%.

how we do it, either pulls us toward the future and pulls the future toward us, or further separates humanity from the future. Work is indeed sacred, and a component part of desiring the kingdom to come, connected not just to this world but to the age to come.

Putting the two aspects of work together, work as related to creation and also to new creation, suggests that work is related to stewarding the world as we have it and enabling it to come to a new, more whole place. Certain spheres of employment yield themselves to this easier than others; conversely, some activity intrinsically works against fulfilling this goal; whereas most work can move in either direction, being dependent on how a person engages with the work.

As followers of Christ, we are to be those who are looking to see how we position ourselves in our work and can be present there for redemptive purposes. If we are unable to act in that way we probably should ask if we should be there at all. Just earning money is not the biblical bottom line, for earning money does not define an activity as work.

Work - people

I suggest that the first 'bottom line' is the impact on people that any work has. In the first volume, I wrote that Jesus was willing to lose money rather than people. If the bottom line is defined by money, we will lose people either in a very visible way where they no longer are needed and the business needs to be streamlined, or in a less visual way where the result is that they lose sight of who they are and so lose something of their humanity.

There is no prohibition concerning making a profit in Scripture. Indeed, the concept of making more money than one needs in order to be generous is very clear. In the Pauline exhortation in Ephesians 4:28 we read,

Anyone who has been stealing must steal no longer,
but must work, doing something useful with their
own hands, that they may have something
to share with those in need.

The reversal that Paul suggests is complete. The former thief is no longer to steal (take what is not his / hers) but to work so that they might be able to give (what now is theirs) to others so that those people might then receive what was not theirs! What is described is a total reversal, and in putting that perspective forward, the creation of a surplus is what is anticipated.

Thus profit is not an issue, but when it is the bottom line we have an issue.

Excessive storing up of wealth

The age to come, the one we are preparing for, and the one that we are preparing the materials for, will not be an age when there will be segregation along financial lines. Yet this age has increasingly sown into that financial divide. In closing this chapter, one that had to be written, let me simply ask how we should best sow into that glorious future. If I am privileged to own my own house, should I pursue an even bigger stake in bricks and mortar? Should I look to store up more for myself with a pension scheme that will only increase the money distortions of society? Should I look to leave money to my descendants so that they might have the potential of moving further up the scale than I was able to?

Hard questions? Or looking at the reality that there is an age to come, how should we live in that light of that?

What remains clear is the concept of simply encouraging believers to rise to the top 3% of the mountain of influence without any critique of the existence of the 'mountain', could indeed release an influence, but the influence might not be an influence for the kingdom. The mountain remaining is not a signpost of the age to come.

Contentment - the legitimate container

If language surrounding the original sin ('saw-desired-consumed') summarises consumerism, and the history that follows that first event bears witness to the destructive path, wisdom tells us that consumerism is not a healthy container for issues surrounding money and possessions. The one with excessive wealth that has achieved that wealth through consumerism is in danger of 'gaining the whole world but losing their soul', and meanwhile, the one who has suffered due to exploitative consumerism is totally dehumanised, and might also battle with the belief and desire that gaining a portfolio of possessions is the gateway to happiness.

Poverty is not a blessing, and many have suffered that curse as the Western world has refused to address the roots of the deep global inequalities. The writer in Proverbs seemed to hit the balance with his (her?) prayer:

> *Two things I ask of you, Lord;*
> *do not refuse me before I die:*
> *Keep falsehood and lies far from me;*
> *give me neither poverty nor riches,*
> *but give me only my daily bread.*
> *Otherwise, I may have too much and disown you*
> *and say, 'Who is the Lord?'*
> *Or I may become poor and steal,*
> *and so dishonour the name of my God.*

> **—** *(Prov. 30:7-9)* **—**

Neither riches nor poverty. Consumerism with its voice of 'never enough', 'one more thing and then I will have enough'!

Or contentment.

Here are a few New Testament Scriptures outlining contentment as the valid container for what we have:

But if we have food and clothing,
we will be content with that.

— (1 Tim. 6:8) —

Keep your lives free from the love of money and
be content with what you have, because God has said,
"Never will I leave you; never will I forsake you."

— (Heb. 13:5) —

I am not saying this because I am in need,
for I have learned to be content whatever the
circumstances. I know what it is to be in need,
and I know what it is to have plenty.
I have learned the secret of being content in any
and every situation, whether well fed or hungry,
whether living in plenty or in want.

— (Phil. 4:11-12) —

The words of Paul, 'I have learned', indicate that this is not a normal state of affairs, but an attitude that has to grow within us. Thankfulness for what we have, or perhaps better put, thankfulness that God remembers us, is a necessary antidote to both anxiety (Phil. 4:6) and worry (Matt. 6:31-34).

Early on, after moving to Spain, we were able to buy an apartment. A neighbour came, complete with pen and paper, and wanted to know how much the apartment had cost and how much we had spent on it. He carefully noted down the figures and added them up. At the end of the addition, he put his hand on his heart saying to us that we are very rich, but he was a poor man! We decided to give him the figures as we wanted to be open, after all if we want people to be open to the Gospel but we cannot be open about something as shallow as money, how genuine is that?

At that time we owned an apartment, he owned five properties; we had just bought a vehicle having been without one for the previous five years, he owned two cars; our expenses meant that we could no longer return to the UK and purchase even half the property we had sold there. Had we both been using a calculator that day, I think maybe I would have proclaimed to him that he was rich. But as he finished his sentence, I simply replied with, 'Yes, you are correct'. We are incredibly rich in monetary terms, for there are so many who struggle to put food on the table or a roof over their heads. However, possessions and value of property are not the true measurements. To be rich in contentment cannot be measured and should never be swapped for 'one more thing' and... discontentment.

We do not live in a perfect world, and we await the age to come. While living in the in-between time, while we inhabit this imperfect world, we have to make compromises, yet we cannot simply compromise while refusing to look at the issues that pollute our world. Mammon and consumerism have been here since the beginning, but will not be here at the end. We live in between those two points. If we allow ourselves to be dragged back then, for sure, we are not of those who are contributing to the transformation of this world, and the preparation of the next.

An addendum on shareholding

Money, and what we do with it, is so complex. Put money into a pension fund, and one often loses control over where that money is invested in order to get a return. Even under many national banking laws put money in a bank and the money is 'owned' by the bank, who promise to return a payment upon demand. If one is comfortable in investing directly in shares, the question raised is 'but where?' Thankfully there are ethically based investment funds often available that can alleviate the conscience.

Perhaps a guideline might be to look to invest in sectors that are helping contribute to a future that one desires to see. A 'sow where you want the world to go' approach. If we consider investing simply where there is the best financial return, I doubt we would be among those who are seeking to overturn the spirit of Mammon that has, thus far, had a loud voice in shaping the future.

I have come across companies who operate with a 1-1-1 approach; where employees can give 1% of their allotted time (that is contracted to the company) for free into voluntary work for society; or the company gives 1% of the profits back to society; or 1% of product is given away freely - a small contribution to a different world.

None of the above might be perfect, but the investment that is made with a future perspective carries something redemptive. Though we are not looking for the perfect solution, we do not simply accept that there is nothing we can do, but are exercised to find a redemptive response.

CHAPTER 3

DIRTY FEET

I am very grateful for the pull of Scripture to think and live at a different level to this world. Paul said:

> *Do not conform to the pattern of this world,*
> *but be transformed by the renewing of your mind.*
> *Then you will be able to test and approve what God's*
> *will is - his good, pleasing and perfect will.*
>
> **- *(Rom. 12:2)* -**

The pattern of this world is present every day, in both explicit and implicit ways, and with this pressure being ever-present we can easily drop off into a sleep where we do not even register how we are being affected. To counteract that tranquilising effect, we have to engage with an ongoing renewing of our minds.

I am equally grateful that there is a deep pragmatism that comes through the pages of Scripture. We see it in the Law, where we do not have the (absolute) will of God revealed, but often see requirements that encourage people to act and move in the right direction. The biblical commentary on slavery is a classic example. Declaring that humanity is created in God's image there can be no higher implicit condemnation of slavery, yet the practice is accommodated all the way through the pages, and even Jesus does not speak out against its ills. However, one aspect that remains is that there is a relentless redemptive push toward something better as we follow the biblical trajectory.

That trajectory means it is sometimes difficult to know if we are being 'biblical'. We can tick the 'I am biblical' box if we define being biblical as finding a few Scriptures that we are comfortable with... particularly when they also comply with our already pre-formed views! But if we follow the trajectory, a trajectory that we have, many times, to work out where it is headed, then being biblical is much more than conforming to some texts. It is being submitted to, and participating as an active agent in, enabling the story to reach its goal. Thankfully those who were abolitionists did not stop at the text but followed the narrative.

There is a phrase that can be useful, but one I do not like, which is 'the lesser of two evils'. I understand the meaning of it but do not like the negativity contained in it. I much prefer the encouragement to find the most redemptive way forward. Redemptive might not mean 'perfect' for it is very difficult to unscramble eggs and put them back in their shells. Redemption does not work like that. God comes to every situation and is actively involved in working toward the best possible outcome.

Compromise

God is a compromiser. But a redemptive compromiser. I know first-hand that he compromises, for he walks with me! That definitively shows he is willing to compromise. I understand the sentiment that God is holy and cannot look on sin, but I am glad that that sentiment is only semi-true. Religion has a problem with sin, and the solution provided is guilt. God is a companion to sinners, and the solution on offer is redemption.

When Jesus washed the disciples' feet, it was not something he acted out, but, with a wrapped towel, it was yet again a revealing of who he eternally was. The shock that he would do this was too much for Peter, for in that culture it was not possible to insist that a Hebrew slave carry out such a task. The cleansing by Jesus was essential, so Peter then went overboard in his response, with a request for a total bath. Jesus explained that (and I paraphrase) once we come to follow him we are clean, but where we have to walk is dusty, and our feet will get dirty. We simply need to have that dust washed off on a regular basis.

Where we tread, if we follow Jesus, is full of the dust of death. Dust that has never had the life of God breathed into it, never been humanised. Devoid of the kenotic life of God, that selfless giving of life, the default consumption of fellow humans all but inevitably results. If we do not tread there, how will it ever be open to the breath of God? And if we tread there but do not stay focused, how will we ensure that we are not eventually encased in layers of such dust?

Life is a compromise. Perhaps we might be able to relocate to a holy commune and avoid the pollution of the world, but in that very act we will be in very real danger of acting in a non-God-like way, for God came and inhabited our world, who in Jesus came and took up residence 'in our neighbourhood'. Escape is not an option. And if we cannot escape, we also cannot keep our feet clean. Living for Jesus (a choice) and having dirty feet (the result of the choice) go together.

The previous chapter might have seemed a little heavy, and I am glad for that. I believe we have to ask the hard questions. We have to connect the dots, and if we do not subject monetary issues to a biblical critique, it will not be long before we are indeed conformed to the pattern of this world.

I have often reflected on Paul's optimism. We read in 2 Cor, 6:10 *'having nothing, and yet possessing everything'.*

I have also turned the phrase around as it fits my situation more accurately. 'Having everything, and yet possessing nothing'. I might not literally have 'everything', but to have a comfortable place that can be called 'home' comes close to having everything. It does not matter how much I have, whether it is measured as a few things or everything, for the question remains for me to answer. That question being, 'how now am I to live in such a way that others can possess what I have?'[1]

If we want to see a new politics in the land, then whether or not we are willing to play football in the street with some 8-year-olds might well be the key. If we want keys to the nation, to give neighbours a set of keys saying our home is your home, saying 'use it when you wish' might well be, not simply a generous act, but a necessary one, particularly if the neighbours are not believers. If we want them to share our faith, perhaps we need to share our resources with them. I have discovered that we are not normally too far from the answers to our prayers. The answers are often closer to us than we realise, and they inevitably will be present to us in human form, in how we relate to those who are loved by heaven, and how we steward whatever we have for their benefit.

Life is a compromise, but we are to be involved redemptively. In the same way that God walks with us, journeying redemptively with us, we are to be involved in such a way that something good comes forth. Applying this to the subject matter of the last chapter; all of work is to be entered into so that we find what is redemptive in it. That redemptive element will centre on what enables others to find their destiny, and likewise, as we enable others, we will experience a return as we also move forward in that same direction.

---

1 By this, I am not suggesting that we allow all and sundry to cross boundaries and take what is not theirs. That would be to encourage and even facilitate them to be less-than-human. Robbery is what is taken; gift is what is given, and in the culture of the New Testament it seems 'gift' was not an act of charity, but a considered and generous response to enable someone else to move toward their destiny.

In the first volume, I wrote about the nature of sin as to be less than human, and to act in a non-human way. The results are all forms of alienation, as the verdict over that way of living is 'to fall short of the glory of God'. Glory is revealed to us in the face of the Human, Jesus. The involvement with people, the inevitable experience of getting our feet dirty, is a path toward glory, a redemptive path toward a greater level of humanisation.[2]

The path to glory

There are three words that are connected in Scripture. The word 'glory' is preceded by the word 'suffering' and the bridge between them is one of those undefinable words: 'time'.

And the God of all grace,
who called you to his eternal glory in Christ,
after you have suffered a little while.

━ *(1 Peter 5:10)* ━

For our light and momentary troubles
are achieving for us an eternal glory
that far outweighs them all.

━ *(2 Cor. 4:17)* ━

Did not the Messiah have to suffer these things
and then enter his glory?

━ *(Luke 24:26)* ━

---

2 Our feet become dirty, not because the people we touch are dirty, but the context, 'the world' or 'world system' as named by Scripture, has a default bias of dehumanising as many as possible. Those who are, willing or unwitting, agents of this might 'prosper' but the many who are simply in the system are resisted from discovering their destiny.

We love the word 'glory', though we have often only defined it as something unearthly, something transcendent. There is, of course, a transcendent element to it but the word is very earthy, very human.

Suffering is a reality, sometimes ever so painfully evident, but even when it is not present at a visible level, we will experience pressure as we seek to outwork in every situation what it means to be redemptive. It will require that we are willing to put our own reputation, self-comfort and success on the line. There will always be a measure of personal pressure in not being conformed to the pattern of this age.

Into any suffering, that results from engaging redemptively, there comes heaven's promise that we are on the path to glory. We have all asked, and children seem to have asked from eternity past, the same question, 'Are we nearly there yet?' The time question.

There is glory, glory to come when the ultimate timeline is completed. There is also glory in the here and now as we learn to hold on and press in for the changes that are needed to bring health in our world. The one we seek to follow, Jesus, travelled the same path. He grew toward that place of being truly human through what he suffered. Once that growth was complete, he became something to us all, the source of salvation. The Hebrew writer captures this with the use of the term 'perfect'. The writer holding to the sinlessness of Jesus draws out that the path of learning how to respond to the challenges of life is what brought Jesus to maturity. Jesus came to the place of the ultimate outpouring of life for all, and in the language of these volumes, he truly manifested the eternal nature of God as one who was truly a mature human.[3]

---

3 Two example texts from Hebrews:
[God made] the pioneer of their salvation perfect through what he suffered (Heb. 2:10).
He learned obedience from what he suffered and, once made perfect, he became the source of eternal salvation for all who obey him (Heb. 5:8,9).

Glory revealed at the cross. Eternal glory revealed in time and space. The glory of God. The glory that humanity created in the image of God was destined to grow toward, the glory that is seen when life is selflessly outpoured to benefit others, to enable their destiny to be unlocked.

Time, indicative of a journey, is what was needed for the one who was without sin to arrive at maturity. How much more will that be true for us. We, though, can take hope, for we are being changed from one degree of glory to another as we respond to the destiny of being conformed to Jesus' image (2 Cor. 3:18; Rom. 8:28-30). A path that we are on, that one day will be completed, becoming 'like him' when we see him as he is.

It is not possible, nor desirable, that everyone has a job that can be squeaky clean as far as perfection is concerned. Maybe careers in the caring professions come closest, but not all are either called in that way nor attracted in that direction. Yet we all have to aspire to connect redemptively into our world, connecting to people and helping provoke whole systems to change orientation toward those who are on the edges, those who are disenfranchised.

If one has surplus money, a bank will often allocate a personal banker to that person. Conversely, if one is struggling, not knowing how to pay a bill, it is very rare for a senior bank employee to give time freely to help that person. Objectively, who needs the personal advice from the expert? An easy illustration, but one that highlights how our world is not orientated toward the disenfranchised but toward the person deemed to be already successful.

It might be hard to be redemptive in every situation, and we all have to be faithful to the conscience that is within us as to how we outwork our contribution to the future in those settings. What we can be sure of is that we all end each day with some dust on our feet. At the end of each day, we can be thankful for the compromising God who was with us. At the start of each new day, we can ask for renewed strength so that we might be among those who are breathing the life of God into the very dust that can so easily pollute.

CHAPTER 4

BUSINESS AS UNUSUAL

Thankfully there has been a significant move away from spirituality being measured by how much we focus on prayer and Scripture-reading, and from the idea of the highest calling being that of 'full-time' Christian-worker. Paul was not simply a tent-maker by trade, but it can be argued that he achieved his biggest city breakthroughs when he was also actively involved in tent-making. Far from seeing those times when he was tent-making as a regrettable fall-back when he could not be supported 'full-time', we probably ought to see those times as essential for the advance of the Gospel and the effective exercise of his apostolic ministry.

Paul never ceased to be an apostle, nor ceased to be full-time. He was always full-time in his service of the Lord, the Gospel and people, and even when in prison he wrote as an apostle. He never described himself as 'a prisoner of Rome with a temporarily suspended calling to be an apostle!'

Life is sacred, and spirituality is not simply measured by so-called spiritual activities, and as life is embraced we will find an increase of God's influence through us extended beyond the life of any congregation that we might associate with. We might need to be cautious about developing a theology of (for example) 'apostles of the marketplace' but the work of laying foundations that relate to Christ and the Gospel certainly needs to be extended beyond the church construct. In the business realm that apostolic gift of laying healthy foundations that enable people to connect to their unique destiny and be healthily joined to others is so needed.

In recent years something that I would consider is a sign has risen in the business world. It goes under various names, one of which is a 'B-corp status'. It is where there is a push away from profit being the sole bottom line purpose for a business, and sets the development of people and care for the environment as the two top factors. It is not afraid of making a profit, but that aspect takes a lesser priority. I hear something in the description that reflects a kingdom of God perspective, and given that it is not explicated from a biblical set of values but is proposed using firm business language, I see it as an example that if we seek, albeit in a small way to honour kingdom values, there will be a positive response from the world.

Gayle and I have a connection to an amazing work in Romania with a group who work mainly among the disenfranchised. It is a costly work, with the founder of the group having given up a profitable legal career to initially work among street-kids. Until recently, he had not had his own private bedroom, as from the beginning of this work he took young men off the street to live in his property, and train them for society. Over the years the work has grown, and amazingly the biggest financial supporters of the work are business people who are not 'believers'.

Lee told us of an amazing conversation between two wealthy people in the aftermath of the 2008 financial crisis. One asked the other if he had any advice as to a good investment in that globally shaky time.

The telephone conversation went as follows:

'There is one place where we have made an investment that gives a proven return, whether the global markets are up or down.'

'And where is that?'

'Romania.'

A short silence ensued, followed by, 'I have not heard of Romania being a solid investment, and to be honest, I did not expect to hear that. Tell me more about the return.'

'We too were surprised but truthfully it has returned, without fail, year on year.'

'What kind of level of return are you talking about?'

'We both know that in the current climate, we are losing sleep wondering what is going to go down next. It is great to make a good financial return, but the real return we are looking for is 'joy'. The joy of knowing we have made a good investment, that we have got it right. I can guarantee you that if you put money in there, it will return to you something greater than money, it will return joy.'

There was a silence at the other end of the phone, followed by a question, 'Do you think you can get us an opening?'

Joy! Romans 14:17 comes to mind at this point.

> *For the kingdom of God is not a matter of eating*
> *and drinking, but of righteousness, peace*
> *and joy in the Holy Spirit.*

The kingdom of God cannot be measured by physical (economic) responses, but in making right choices, choices that result in sleep at night... and joy.

It is possible, and I believe it is the intention of God, to set out kingdom values in business that influence the wider world resulting in them receiving some of heaven's fruit.

I have a friend who enjoys playing golf. Often there are those who play with him who do not have faith who say to him that they always enjoy playing with him as they always play some of their best rounds while they are on the course with him. His explanation is along the lines of, 'Of course that is their experience, it is inevitable, as I carry the kingdom of God within.' His expectation is that, as he carries the presence of God, it is inevitable that others will be blessed who come within his vicinity, with even their golf score being blessed! What an example of positive faith, but it illustrates that true friendship is important. If people can receive us (or maybe I should put that, if we can humbly build a bridge to them, accept them as they are, and be vulnerable with them) they will receive the one who sent us. And if they receive the one who sent us, their golf handicap can shift! Or, probably more importantly, they can experience joy.

We should not over-spiritualise our lives, thinking that everything we do is founded upon 'and then God said to me do this... and that is what I did'. God looks to us to make decisions, for in the very decision-making we grow. With hindsight we might make different choices if we could start again; there are of course wrong choices, but more often there are choices, some of which are better than others, and regardless of the choice we make at any given point in our lives, we rejoice that God was with us, the wonderful compromising redeemer.

Business consultation

It is not uncommon that when a business plateaus a consultation process begins, quite often with a focus on the structures. Proposals are made, and as a result, the structures change. I am sure there is value in that approach, but something that begins with a focus at the personal level, that looks for change to take place inter-relationally and behaviourally, and therefore at a self-perception level, is much more wholesome. At times structures do need to change, but if they change without there being personal changes, the effect does not normally prove to be long term. An understanding of the nature of all corporations is that over time a corporate culture, what we might even term a corporate personality, develops. This corporate personality that develops will eventually become independent, even from the founders that created the business. That independent personality will do everything in its power to survive, and that includes marginalising and if need be, ejecting certain people. A young business is much more flexible than an older established one, as indeed is often the case with a person. The more flexible a business is, the easier it is for that business to continue to serve the goals that were set at the beginning. The older and less flexible, the greater the pressure there is on the people to serve the corporate business without questioning the methodology or direction.

Those insights are boldly outlined in the Scriptural understanding of the city, where the city is both a physical entity and also carries a spiritual identity. Consultations that do not grasp that might provide tools for change but will not be able to process change that will take a business into its next phase of usefulness, as it is not simply the outward form that needs changing but the internal 'spirit'.

Beyond the corporate renewal and bringing in line of the corporate entity to serve, the personal alignment of those involved has to figure at the top of any consultation. So often people and positions are wrongly aligned, with a fixed post that someone has to be fitted into - *square pegs in round holes comes to mind*. Discovering one's gifts and having that match one's job description is not a 'church' issue but a 'life' issue.

Successful people are seldom exempt from personal issues that they have suppressed. The issues might be somewhat hidden within the work context, but they often manifest to the detriment of others within the family environment. Once we refuse to embrace 'success' as being defined by one's job, size of salary, or the like, but understand that we have to see true value as how others are positively impacted through one's life, we will not be looking for quick fix answers. 'Success', biblically, involves a human measurement. Am I truly being human and enabling others to become more human, is the measurement.

Discovering gifts and strengths so that people can be affirmed will only increase the person's contribution, as well as their satisfaction in the workplace. Helping people to remove the masks will bring about inner peace and an ability to work alongside people of difference.

There is so much that someone in touch with the Spirit of God can bring to the business arena, once we prioritise people over profits, and people over structure. The work of humanising is the work of the Spirit, and this should be the clear gift that someone who understands humanity as revealed in Jesus should be able to bring.

The narcissistic spirit

The Mayo Clinic[1] suggest that the signs and symptoms of a narcissistic personality disorder vary but list a helpful set of identifiers:

- Have an exaggerated sense of self-importance.
- Have a sense of entitlement and require constant, excessive admiration.
- Expect to be recognised as superior even without achievements that warrant it.

---

1 The Mayo Clinic website has a helpful summary at:
https://www.mayoclinic.org/diseases-conditions/narcissistic-personality-disorder/symptoms-causes/syc-20366662 (Accessed 30/08/2020). All the bullet points listed here are reproduced from that page (adjusted for British spelling). Used with permission of Mayo Foundation for Medical Education and Research, all rights reserved.

- Exaggerate achievements and talents.
- Be preoccupied with fantasies about success, power, brilliance, beauty or the perfect mate.
- Believe they are superior and can only associate with equally special people.
- Monopolise conversations and belittle or look down on people they perceive as inferior.
- Expect special favors and unquestioning compliance with their expectations.
- Take advantage of others to get what they want.
- Have an inability or unwillingness to recognise the needs and feelings of others.
- Be envious of others and believe others envy them.
- Behave in an arrogant or haughty manner, coming across as conceited, boastful and pretentious.
- Insist on having the best of everything - for instance, the best car or office.

At the same time, people with narcissistic personality disorder have trouble handling anything they perceive as criticism, and they can:

- Become impatient or angry when they don't receive special treatment.
- Have significant interpersonal problems and easily feel slighted.
- React with rage or contempt and try to belittle the other person to make themselves appear superior.
- Have difficulty regulating emotions and behavior.
- Experience major problems dealing with stress and adapting to change.
- Feel depressed and moody because they fall short of perfection.
- Have secret feelings of insecurity, shame, vulnerability and humiliation.

Makes for challenging reading, and please resist putting names to the question I did not ask! However, did you recognise anyone from the list of symptoms? No, please do not answer! Probably we could all suggest a few names, but what makes it somewhat more complicated is that Narcissus is not the mythical figure who had (as I used to think) an unbalanced level of self-love, but his issue was that he was in love with **an image** of himself. At a deeper level, so much of what contributes to this personality disorder is a measure of self-hatred, or, if not self-hatred, at least a level of never having discovered who they really are. The damage has often been done to cause this back in their childhood years, and the damage they can cause to those around them can be enormous.

A trained psychotherapist, who was also serving as an ordained Anglican minister, explained to me the aspect I mentioned above, of Narcissus being in love with an image of himself. It was due to this aspect, he suggested, that it was often very difficult to meet and relate to many leaders (in church or business) as the person they would introduce to others would not be their true self but the image that they project. A successful image is not biblical success. Helping people embark on a process of self-discovery, self-acceptance, of being human goes much deeper than working as an expert who brings about structural change.

There has to be a voluntary unmasking for this false image to be exposed and the real (human) person to become visible. As numerous successful business entrepreneurs can, without too much effort, identify with several of the symptomatic points highlighted above, a consultant often has to focus on helping the entrepreneur come to understand their damaging behaviour. If a Spirit-led consultant is not focused first on working to maximise profits but maximising a culture that releases destiny, either the entrepreneur will quickly show the exit door to the consultant or an action-packed process will begin![2]

---

2 Once we think beyond the narrow world of evangelism, the commission to 'disciple the nations' and 'baptising them' opens a huge world of mission.

Entrepreneurship and pay scales

The entrepreneurial gift is remarkable. That person can see a possibility where someone else can see nothing positive in the situation. The gift is strong, therefore the entrepreneur is often weak in a number of other areas, and hence for long-term success the development of an effective team becomes key. Without a developed team, the entrepreneur can bring something to birth, then make choices that destroy the very corporate entity, with the cycle repeated numerous times in their lifetime.

The entrepreneur becomes effective when they see the need to add to the team people with different giftings, and even giftings that will hold in check the direction they wish to head in. There needs to be mutual submission, and one of the key ways to put something in place to facilitate this is to have an 'equal pay, equal say' policy. Businesses need the risk-taking entrepreneurial spirit for without that being present, the business will not succeed. And, yet, the business is likely to fail if it is shaped only by the entrepreneur.

In so much of this chapter, I have tried to be practical and been pushed to write into areas where I do not carry a great expertise, but in doing so, I have sought to take the principles outlined earlier and apply them practically. My suggestions can certainly be improved (and that might mean 'binned' and replaced with other, better, suggestions!). Those with wisdom, please feel free to do so. My plea is that we do not allow an ideology of neoliberalism, capitalism, nor socialism to dictate a shape, but allow the Scriptures to shed insight on all our practices - and also our preferred ideologies. Overwhelmingly the Scriptures address the inner core of our being, asking the ever-pertinent question concerning the tragedy of gaining everything but losing one's soul.

I am writing this series of books during the pandemic lockdown that I and others have suggested is a sign of a global reset. If that be true, or only partially true, the landscape will become remarkably open to new ideas and fresh entrepreneurship. If what rises enhances, albeit imperfectly, the release of the gifts and destiny of others, it will truly contribute to the new creation reality that is here. I suspect that the new ventures that I anticipate arising will not make it into the world of multi-nationals that dictate to governments. That realisation has disappointed me, and that disappointment has been acute when viewing honest people losing employment and businesses closing down in this period of time, and at the same time noting the huge increase of personal wealth by some of those involved in the (often) dehumanising multi-nationals. However, I am coming to realise that I should not see the stark contrast as failure but to embrace the kingdom movement that begins in the wilderness. Small changes will together act as a leverage point to shift what seems to currently dominate the whole landscape.

CHAPTER 5

HEALTHY EDUCATION

Many good-hearted people, including many believers, have pursued careers in either the health or education sectors. And for good reason too, for those two areas are deeply engaged in the humanisation process.

I appreciate that there is something of a divide between the North American approach and the European on health and on education, so just a quick note here before proceeding. I have always considered that as many people as possible should be offered the best opportunity, so the best possible health care and education should be offered to one and all, as far as is possible, regardless of the financial resources they have. I see those as rights (and not merely privileges), that maybe cannot be demanded, but can be fought for by those who are among the privileged.[1] I do not see good health care and good education as privileges that should have to be paid for.

---

1 I am writing of my personal perspective and am also aware that many 'ideals' are not possible. Choices have to be made that are compromises, between what is ideal and what is actually possible. I also acknowledge that what are termed 'handouts' to those who have contributed nothing are considered unhelpful. Legislation is into a complex world; thus I have used the phrase 'as far as possible' in the paragraph.

It is also interesting that many missional approaches use education or health as a genuine gift to a community, or as a means to gain favour in order to 'preach the Gospel'. If the latter is the motivation, but those people also do not believe in universal health care and education, surely the use of education and health as a means in to a community lacks something in integrity?

By requiring payment, it is elevating money to a place of dictatorial rule rather than placing financial resources in the role of servant (and stewardship on behalf of those who do not have the same access to those resources). Although not directly related to the argument of private vs public availability, it is clear that Jesus did not offer healing nor his teaching only to those who could afford it.[2] I am not asking for those who take another approach to understand my perspective on this, but I hope though that what I write will be applicable also to those who do not share my view.

These two areas of health and education are almost made for believers. We believe in a healing God who is moved with compassion, and there are repeated commands to teach the next generation in Scripture. Because these two realms are so close to the heart of God I suggest that those who work in them and the very systems that have been put in place are separated out for some very specific attack. The closer we align to God's values, consciously or by default of what we are involved in, the more we will become a focus for resistance. That resistance might come in personal form, but even then the real resistance is 'spiritual' for we do not wrestle against 'flesh and blood'.[3]

To live at some level as Christ lived, in other words, to be self-giving and placing the needs of others centre-focus, is to make oneself something of a target. To seek to contribute to the health of someone else, often at personal cost and at times at personal risk, or to partner with children so that they might be better equipped for the future is to positively engage in the humanisation of others. I consider that

---

2 I think we also have to consider how we make what we have available as a gift that can bring about remuneration from those who can, and yet be given freely to those who cannot afford it. We cannot change everything, but this does not mean that we simply follow in the path of insisting that everything is carried out on a commercial and transactional basis. 'Gift' is a Pauline theme; it is not understood as charity, but as a contribution given freely that calls the recipient to rise up to their destiny.

3 By 'spiritual' I do not mean it will not manifest in a tangible way, but that there are energising powers that will animate / seek to keep the situation ever present. We can interpret that as 'personal forces' or as energising principles; the result is the same.

demonstrates something of a friendship to Christ, and therefore will put that person at enmity 'to the world' (John 15:18-21).

The very institutions, the health and education systems, are always liable to being subverted due to their positive aspirations. One of the commonest ways for that to occur is the pressure to set goals that are not for the benefit of the clients - Medical institutions that have to cut corners, pharmaceutical companies who seek to monopolise the market, or staff that have to work unreasonable hours so that expenses can be minimised. Likewise, in education there has always been a danger that the system is set in such a way that it does not meet the needs of the students, but works only for some, while sadly causing damage to those who cannot fit. In both areas, the focus moves away from the person. Sounds familiar? The work of the demonic is to dehumanise and to institutionalise people, with the institution being served and those within it being devalued.

Learning to work in the fallen systems for the benefit of people is a truly redemptive task. Teachers who see the child not according to their ethnic background, gender, nor according to the value they are to the system, are gifts from heaven. Teachers who can 'see' the child with all that lies ahead are worth their weight in gold. Teachers who prophesy, not simply by word, but by working alongside the child draw out their unique gifts and prepare that child to make their contribution to the world, are the teachers who are responding to the call of God to enter the realm of education with the Spirit. They are those who contribute to training up the child in the way **they** should go, discovering the child's gifts and matching any curriculum to the child rather than the child to the curriculum.

Care workers who truly value the person and thus are able to help that person see themselves a little more accurately carry something from heaven that the health system, so often, does not allow to happen. They are able to reflect something of Jesus who confronted Simon the Pharisee with the question, 'Do you see this woman?'

(Luke 7:44). Simon had not seen the woman but had categorised her according to his religious label. He saw a 'sinner', a prostitute. Systems carry labels, and they categorise. Jesus sees people.

The caring and education areas might be a good fit for those who have been touched by the redemptive love of Jesus, but they will inevitably also be two areas where opposition will be found.

All kingdom activity will be opposed. This is part of what it is to 'make up what is lacking in the afflictions of Christ'. The 'mark of the beast' (666, Rev. 13:18) is not some theoretical tattoo but manifests in very concrete situations where conformity to the system is required. Put people first, act in a way that insists the structures are here to serve people and careers can be put in jeopardy. For such people it will not be uncommon for rumours to arise, as (spiritual but very real) opposition manifests against those who push back against any dehumanising system. Integrity, honesty and persistence will be needed, but the value to the here and now, and the contribution to the 'then and here' will be very hard to measure. Certainly, heaven will respond with a huge 'well done'.

Health, education and more

There are many other sectors where people make their contribution that are deemed a 'good fit' for believers. Too many to mention, and many in realms that I am far from qualified to comment on. Two that quickly come to mind follow.

Environmentalists who call us to account for what we are doing to the planet, to God's creation. Those who sound a warning, but also bring that eschatological element that what is here is to be renewed not destroyed. Although some Christians understandably react to language such as 'mother earth', one might argue the Bible itself comes close to that understanding when it states that we are formed from the dust of the ground. This is also the language used in Isaiah when the hope of resurrection is expressed:

But your dead will live, Lord;
their bodies will rise -
let those who dwell in the dust
wake up and shout for joy -
your dew is like the dew of the morning;
the earth will give birth to her dead.

— *(Is. 26:19)* **—**

The earth giving birth! Of course this is poetic language, but it pushes us so far away from the abusive view of the earth's resources simply being there to be exploited.[4]

We face dire warnings from the scientific world with the blame laid at the feet of humanity. That voice of blame should sound familiar to those of the Christian faith, for we read very early on that the 'earth will be cursed because of you.' Believers who are active in the realm of creation care, or active in protests relating to the environment are resonating both with the early chapters of Genesis and the hope that there will indeed be a renewal of all creation, expressed eloquently in the Johannine language of 'I saw a new heaven and a new earth' (Revelation 21:1).

Another realm that dovetails easily with the hope of the Gospel is shown through the lives of those who are engaged in the costly work of reconciliation and mediation, whether that be expressed in reconciliation at the level of interpersonal relationships through to that of international conflicts. Those that call for resolution that 'might is right' can never bring about; those that understand relationships can be restored; and those that understand that sometimes the way forward is a good 'divorce'. Those who approach hostile environments, entering it humbly, prayerfully but knowing

---

4 Scripture avoids the deification of creation, but does ascribe personality to creation. Creation has a voice (Ps. 19:1,2), it groans waiting for liberation (Rom. 8:19-22), and the land comes to aid the woman being persecuted (Rev. 12:16). The relational connection between creation and humanity is very close.

that God enters those situations with them. Such people and their efforts fit easily into the arc of justice that is within the heart of God, and is in the DNA of God's creation.[5]

---

5 Theodore Parker (1810-1860), an advocate for abolition, and one convinced of its inevitable success, said, 'I do not pretend to understand the moral universe; the arc is a long one, my eye reaches but little ways; I cannot calculate the curve and complete the figure by the experience of sight; I can divine it by conscience. And from what I see I am sure it bends towards justice'. (Others, including Martin Luther King Jr, and Barack Obama have used Parker's words in speeches since).

CHAPTER 6

LAW, ORDER AND JUSTICE

Right and wrong. This appeals to many Christians, and to some it is very simple; there are laws that should be applied, for 'righteousness exalts a nation' (Proverbs 14:34). In a previous chapter I outlined how challenging the application of this is, for when we ask, 'And what laws do we wish to see on the statute books?' we should quickly realise how difficult the application is. The 'do not murder' law, or the 'do not be angry' one? Legislation against adultery or against lust? By saying, 'But I say to you', Jesus exposed that even Torah law was not absolute. Israel as a unique nation in covenant with God, received laws that were less than true kingdom values and so, at some level, were compromises.

Many governments have laws that go further than the laws we read in the Old Testament, and also governments have laws that do not go as far as the ones given to Israel. There are no laws on the statute books of any nation that I am aware of that prohibit the wearing of clothing made from different materials, or that the way to deal with rebellious children would be to get some older men to beat them at the entry point to the community! Conversely, we know that there are governments that legislate against slavery, thus going further than the laws that God gave to Israel. Some national laws do not go as far as Old Testament law; some go further. Old Testament law only takes us so far; giving some guiding principles but also applying those principles to the agrarian life of the theocracy known as Israel.

Yet even when we seek to draw out the principles from the ancient laws of Israel, which ones do we draw out? Should we look for harsh, but fair punishments based on 'an eye for an eye' or do we look to (as God did) cover and protect even the murderer?[1]

Christians have been very quick to locate their values around one or two causes that shape their votes. And if reduced to one issue the 'protect the unborn' plea normally wins the debate. Yet that issue is so complex. A simple argument of 'protect the unborn' can easily ignore the wider issues of education, poverty and misogyny that contribute to the statistics. Is the Christian response to vote from behind the safety of the four walls, or to look for a shift on the issues that are 'upstream' that have polluted the waters?[2] And using the label 'pro-life' can be very misleading although very comforting to those who believe in the sanctity of life. However, does pro-life only extend to the first nine months? What about being pro-life for the years beyond the womb? In some places, those who are 'pro-life' are anything but pro-life when it comes to the support of the military, where it seems the right thing is to be pro-life for the unborn but to refuse to see the life of a person from another land, who might have a different faith, as someone made in the image of God, who Jesus died for so that they might live. The issues are far from simple and clear-cut.

The pro-life legislation is much wider than the abortion issue and regardless of one's personal views finding what is the appropriate

---

1 Genesis 4:15.

2 It does not fit the reality to suggest that stronger anti-abortion laws reduce the level of abortions. Issues, such as abortion, again indicate how our feet become ever so dirty. I appreciate that abortion as murder is an overwhelming conviction for many, but I am also aware of politicians who are 'pro-life' but see the way forward as seeking to address the contributing factors.

legislation on the statute books is not so easy. Perhaps we have to find a messy way where our personal convictions and the realisation of what might be good as public legislation could well differ, with the public legislation being far from perfect. Believers who serve in the public realm of law-making will probably be caught in that dilemma many times, over this issue and others.

I think there are times we (I include myself in the 'we') want legislation that will make us comfortable; legislation that will control societal practice in a direction that we approve of, and legislation that will not inconvenience us at all. Surely the God who was highly inconvenienced by us desires more from his representatives?

The world we live in is not the world that is to come; the ethics for a follower of Jesus cannot be imposed on those who do not claim to follow him. And navigating a way forward that accepts compromise, while not compromising personally, needs the wisdom of God, and I suspect individual believers will outwork that differently.

Law, in all its forms, cannot legislate for every situation, and Christians involved in the areas of law, government and order will quickly find themselves having to respond to many situations that are not as clear as one would like. Again this illustrates that the call on the believer is truly an 'intercessory' call, standing in an uncomfortable position to bring about something healthier.

What party should I vote for?

What a great question! And hopefully, having skirted around the thorny issue of 'pro-life' in the previous paragraphs, I have said enough to dissuade us from thinking that there is a 'Christian party'. For some believers, the 'pro-life' (narrowly defined) stance, or the policy on marriage, of a particular party will be enough to get their vote. Responding personally, I have to consider wider issues than the 'morality' ones. My vote will go with the party whose policies

I cannot endorse totally, and I suspect that if someone votes for the opposite 'wing' they will also realise their vote also was not for the 'Christian' option.

If sin is at heart to fail to be human and to dehumanise others, I think a huge consideration will be to ask what policies will help create an environment where the greatest number of people can be humanised. I certainly do not consider that we should vote along the lines of what will make our personal lives easier. As a believer in Jesus, I might also have to defend the rights of those of other faiths and should not look for a government to ensure we, as Christians, are protected at the expense of others.

I suspect that the majority of my readers are among the privileged of society, and as such what we do with those privileges is important. Preserve and further protect our privileges, or look at the situation of those who are without privileges, and act toward a greater equalisation?

Believers who enter the public arena of politics are brave in the extreme if they enter there to represent Jesus. In representing Jesus, they might not always be the recipients of a 'well done' from the church. If they enter that realm to represent Christianity (or the version that has developed in the West, and been exported around the world), then they might keep the majority of the church happy, but might I suspect in the process dehumanise countless thousands.

Restorative justice

How do we understand justice? How do we understand the cross? Was the cross a transaction that allowed us to go free, on the basis that Jesus was punished in our place? Or did the cross reconcile us to God, restoring the broken relationship?

In many countries, the prison system is broken. Statistically, we know that those who have offended and been imprisoned, once released, often offend again; that a higher percentage of those in prison are illiterate than in wider society. Such statistics simply illustrate that a 'punishment that fits the crime' approach will never heal the issues in a broken and unfair society. Viewed as law-breakers, the only question that is asked is what punishment fits the crime. Surely the cross of Jesus, where the glory of God is revealed speaks into this situation. It starts with the value of the person, the value of the 'sinner'. Judgement is not at the forefront, but love that sees the person, not the criminal. The goal of the cross is not punishment but restoration. For this reason, although working in a fallen setting, believers who work in the criminal justice sphere will seek to act as far as they can to enable the restoration of relationships, rather than a simple punishment of the wrongdoer.

I do not think that there are many negative definitions in Scripture. Faithfulness in marriage is not achieved when a person avoids sleeping with someone they are not in covenant relationship with. Faithfulness is not the absence of something but is measured by the presence of positive qualities. Not telling a lie might be a good place to start, but we are required to leave a transparent self-disclosed reality.[3] Likewise, justice is not fulfilled when a 'suitable' punishment is given, but when something happens positively that brings a measure of repair to the damage caused. Law and punishment might restrict the effects in a wider society, but it will always take more than restrictions to bring about healing.

Not such a good fit

Our world is fallen, and at times so badly fallen. The law courts can punish the person who has stolen a loaf of bread but show how weak it is when being unable to call a multinational corporation to

---

3 God's faithfulness is reflected in the positive response to our faithfulness. S/he takes responsibility for our errors. There is a positive move toward the other party, rather than the avoidance of breaking a vow. In Ephesians we read that we are to, '[P]ut off falsehood and speak truthfully to your neighbour, for we are all members of one body' (Ephes. 4:25). This goes so much further than not telling a lie!

account. I can be prosecuted for withholding tax that I owe, but the large corporation can negotiate, even dictate, how much (how little) tax they will pay.

If education and health are a close fit as a career choice for believers, then the whole realm of law, order and government might be a good fit for Christians who insist on what is right, but those realms will prove to be a tough place to be located for those whose goal is to follow Jesus. A challenging place to enter, but one where extra grace will be supplied if we enter with weakness.

Ekklesia! Carrying a vision for a transformed world, yet knowing that this world is, and will continue to be, a fallen world. Ekklesia, engaged redemptively, seeking to leave evidence of the justice of heaven wherever people from that movement have been present.

Law-breaking?

'Obey the powers, for they are ordained of God' (loose translation of Romans 13:1), is used to hold us all in check, but it is doubtful if that is what Paul intended. The passage cannot be taken in an absolute fashion that will never have any exceptions.[4] The immediate context forbids taking a violent stance against powers,[5] but the verses that follow (our chapter 13) are contextually written and contain a measure of irony within them. The command to pay taxes was written in the historical context when there was much debate and

---

4 One of the early Christian martyrs, Polycarp, makes it clear how he read the passage in Romans. Replying to the Roman proconsul he said, "You I might have considered worthy of a reply, for we have been taught to pay proper respect to rulers and authorities appointed by God, as long as it does us no harm; but as for these, I do not think they are worthy, that I should have to defend myself before them." Polycarp adds some provisos: whether the authorities are worthy and if it does not do harm to the Christian faith.

5 Romans 12:14-21. It seems false to claim that Jesus and the early Christians were pacifists, if by that we mean they did not resist. Resist they did, but the resistance was of a non-violent resistance. The activist, Gandhi, in resisting the British oppressive rule took inspiration from the practice of Jesus.

public unrest with regard to taxation within the city of Rome.[6] This is not to suggest that there is no application of these verses beyond the historical context, but to indicate that the letter is written to a specific situation at a specific time. Then with regard to the seeming endorsement of the use of the 'sword' by the civil powers, there is quite some irony in what he writes. The emperor at the time, Nero, made the claim that he did not need to use the sword to enforce order, such was the benevolent and developed rule that he exercised.[7] Right in the heart of the chapter Paul writes:

> *But if you do wrong, be afraid,*
> *for rulers do not bear the sword for no reason.*
>
> ▬ *(Rom. 13:4)* ▬

In that verse, there is a little side-swipe at the lie Imperial power tells. Comply, and there will be no 'sword', but for those who do not comply? (And given that Paul was probably executed under Nero's rule shows the irony in the claim that rulers only exercise the sword to punish the wrongdoer!) Any reading of Romans 13 needs to be placed alongside a reading of Revelation 13 where the true nature of Imperial rule is exposed, and all kinds of marginalisation takes place for the non-compliant ones.

Shakespeare wrote an oft-repeated line, (from the play, Hamlet).

> *'The lady doth protest too much, methinks'.*

---

6 The Roman historian, Tacitus, writes of this unrest as coming to a head in 58AD; Paul's letter to the Romans is normally dated 56 or 57AD.

7 The Roman philosopher Seneca (4BC - 65AD) said of Nero that his gift was of 'a state unstained by blood, and your prideful boast that in the whole world you have shed not a drop of human blood is the more significant and wonderful because no one ever had the sword put into his hands at an earlier age'. If only that was the case!

I suggest we might coin a new phrase that 'we, the privileged, do not protest enough'. There is cautious wisdom within those chapters in Romans dealing with life at the centre of the Empire. Advice such as pay what you owe (13:6,7) or to live at peace with all, as far as is possible (12:18). Such advice makes good sense in the context. We might paraphrase it as, 'Choose how you protest for, in your context, any protest will have significant repercussions.' We see the same practical advice regarding marriage in the Corinthian context that Paul gave 'because of the present crisis' (1 Cor. 7:25). Those early Christians living in the seemingly all-powerful world of the Roman empire were indeed living in a time of extreme pressure, and they needed to think carefully about how they responded.[8]

The same practical advice is relevant today, but for those of us whose lives are not threatened by the majority of our actions, we need to consider how best to use that luxury. To protest against persecution, climate crisis and the oppression of voices that challenge the status quo, in certain parts of our globe could well be life-threatening. That is not a reason in itself not to protest in those situations, but any response needs to be taken soberly and wisely. However, in other parts of the world (mine included) the luxury of protesting without the consequence of one's life being threatened means we would have to consider reasons why we would not add our voice and physical presence to those who are protesting and calling for an end to injustice.

Such protest might be seen as 'law-breaking', but the push back against injustice requires a higher allegiance than that of complying. One might suggest that the resurrection of Jesus from the dead was not exactly compliant with Roman or Jewish custom and law! It was indeed a political act against all dominant political power.

---

8 The empire went through many crises, and the years from the early 50s right through to the 'year of the four emperors' (69AD) and the Jewish Wars of 66-70AD were indeed years of concentrated crises. Turbulent times, the end of an era and the beginning of another; in biblical language the end of this period probably marks the end of 'this present age'.

A final note on Christian / sharia law

I am a strong believer that the people who follow Jesus are called to be the redemptive element in the world. This seems to be the implication of Jesus telling them to go and 'disciple nations'. He had risen with all authority, so acting under his instruction they would go with his authority. Carrying authority should be a fearful thing. If we have authority, we can cause more damage than someone who does not carry that authority. Those involved in the occult might wish a family ill, but if that family learns how to bless those who curse and their faith were to rise through understanding that 'greater is he in us than he who is in the world' ironically the family would become healthier, and healthier thanks to the occult opposition! However, if a parent was always criticising their child, continually finding fault with their every action, the negative effect would be far beyond that which could be brought through occult opposition. The difference between the two examples is that the relational authority multiplies the effect.

I appreciate that there are believers involved in politics and the legal realm that are concerned about the rise of Islam and the imposition of 'sharia' law. My deep concern is that I consider the strength of Islam is that it drinks from the well that Christendom opened up. If we are to act toward others as we wish them to act toward us, I ask what have we done over centuries? A desire to implement 'Christian' legislation and develop a quasi-Christian state, far from restricting the domain covered by sharia law, will actually fuel the potential expansion of it.

Legislation is necessary, but any imposition of law that is focused on favouring us will only strengthen discriminatory law that certain faiths might wish to impose.

I am not in favour of 'sharia' law (though their banking laws are considerably more in line with the kingdom than the ones we have developed!); neither am I in favour of Christian law. Fallen, compromises, tentative redemptive activities. Those are words that come to mind. Maybe we could replace them with an early text,

By the sweat of your brow you will eat your food
until you return to the ground.

Jesus never promised it would be easy but prayed that the Father would not take the disciples out of the world!

CHAPTER 7

MEDIA MATTERS

The media, the release of news, comment and critique are important. Information, insight, telling the story behind the story and holding those in power to account are all part of a healthy media in any society claiming to support freedom of information. The media is often not without bias, with channels and news-media bought and controlled with a political bias.

Once we understand the bias that is involved[1] the ever-constant threat of who controls our destiny becomes real. No longer is the 'mark of the beast' a theory about the end-times but a reality we face. The idea that we are to get to the top and change everything does not resonate with the battle and resistance we face.

The reality is it is very difficult for believers to enter some of these arenas. If we cannot be bought (and so much of the media has been bought), there are many times that our 'face' will simply not fit.

---

1 A certain news corporation on entering the UK market produced a simple newspaper that became the one with the largest circulation. To change the politics of the readers it adopted a policy of targeting working-class males. It used simple language and over decades was famous for its page 3, photographs each day of a scantily-dressed topless woman. The same corporation entering the USA had a different target audience, and positioned itself as supporting 'family values'!

Wisdom, as to where and over what we can compromise; courage over what we cannot compromise! Familiar themes from our earlier chapters.

Communication

God is a communicator. The media picks up on this aspect of who God is. Indeed the Hebrew bible does not argue for the existence of God; it simply proclaims 'And God said'. God is the communicating God, and a God who communicates exists! The devil is also presented as a communicator, entering into dialogue with Eve in the garden with a view of bringing about a distortion of the truth.[2] In response to this fateful dialogue, God comes on the scene to provoke dialogue and self-reflection. The question 'where are you Adam?' was certainly not because God was limited in his ability to play hide and seek! It was because Adam thought he could hide but had not discovered how inadequate he was at playing the game - and not to mention that he was not about to win some fashion show award. Fig-leaves! Really?

Communication involves clear reporting of facts, or facts as they have been observed. The media has a duty to communicate in that way, and is always one of the first areas that any dictatorship wishes to control, as it has to also become the servant of 'telling a lie, make it big, and repeat it'.[3] The position for the media is to help people see, and the strength of our time is the rise of social-media (lack of control) while the weakness of social-media is that falsehoods can be

---

2 The serpent was probably not originally an image for Satan, but the figure for provocative wisdom (cf. 'be as wise as serpents'). In later Jewish writings there is the development of the Satan figure, and this is very common in the early Christian literature. One does not have to believe in a literal devil, but the reality through the personification of a 'something evil' or a 'someone evil' who communicates remains.

3 This process is attributed to Joseph Goebbels, the propaganda minister in the Third Reich government of Hitler.

propagated very easily (lack of control).[4]

Hollywood and films

I was watching the film 'Shawshank Redemption' a number of years ago and was deeply impacted by the exposure of institutionalism. Here were men who had been imprisoned for years and had all the talk of escape and freedom, but when the opportunity came, some of the key players held back. They were institutionalised and trapped. As the film finished I said out loud, 'That's the kind of film Christians should be making.' That was the impact the message had on me. No sooner had those words come out of my mouth than I had the following go through my head, so clear that it could have been an audible voice:

*No, you are wrong. This is not the kind of film
Christians should be making; it is the kind of film
that Christians are responsible to see made.*

I had to reflect on that as it was such a surprise. My original thought was: Christian producer, director, cast etc., probably made in a Christian owned studio... then probably the follow on would be a predominantly Christian audience, and perhaps with the inevitable smaller budget a somewhat inferior final product.

There could be great value in such a film, but that 'audible' thought caused me to see things differently. We should not expect Hollywood, or any equivalent institution, to automatically produce films that are in line with our values. After that experience I realised that we (the body of Christ) are commissioned with 'all authority'. It is

---

4 The documentary, 'The Social Dilemma', shows how the algorithm used means I will be fed items of news that simply confirm my bias. If I have a tendency to a position, I will read only material with that position in it. This means the gap between me and someone of a differing persuasion becomes an ever-increasing chasm. This gets exploited with voter influence at election time, and in the future with the advance of AI it will be a very real possibility to predict where I will go. The very prediction will lead me there!

our responsibility to change the spiritual dynamic that shapes the 'Hollywoods' of this world, and it is our responsibility as to what comes out of that industry. Suddenly my vision, and the level of challenge, was enlarged.

A wider principle

Since that time, I have seen how the principle of the body of Christ being responsible for what is produced applies much wider than the film industry. To take responsibility removes the judgmental approach we so often have, or the drive to produce the Christian alternative at every point. By no means am I suggesting that we simply take this sense of responsibility on and then the film industry is changed! That would be such a pleasant thought, but totally unreal. After all, the garden of Eden had a very healthy environment, but the story tells us the right path was not chosen.

Freedom of choice remains, and that means freedom to choose a wrong path. However, our responsibility seems to be to remove the influences that all but dictate (wrong) choice.

I consider that if the body of Christ took this seriously with prayer and engagement, we could gradually see some wonderful shifts. If we stopped focusing on the internal purity of the church and turned our attention to the world that God loves, we could also enjoy the gifts that are present in our (fallen) world.

Christian media... or media?

There are those who have dedicated their lives to the development of the Christian media, and I am sure it has its place. Indeed I have an aspiration that as the world moves beyond this immediate pandemic, that huge parts of the Christian media could be positioned to help the church reposition itself to be in the world, to focus on being the body of Christ. I suspect that the changes in our world will be huge and the need for a wholesale change of mindset in the church will be absolutely necessary, and Christian media could have an enormous part to play in the repositioning of the body.

If Christian media simply promotes a 'we are a clean alternative, and so there is no need ever for you to be polluted', it would not get my vote! And yet in God, there is always a 'by all means' policy to reach someone.

Purity is not measured by what I avoid, but by what I affect, and this is why in this chapter I have not focused on Christian media. My focus has rather been on the believers who are willing to enter the challenging space of the 'secular' media, who enter there not to christianise it but to make space for the fragrance of Jesus to be present. If the body of Christ ceases to be concerned about its own continued existence (I think there is Someone who will ensure that!) and its own purity through avoidance, then we can anticipate an increase of those who are willing, and able, to stand in this vital and challenging realm of the media.

CHAPTER 8

LET THE SMALL ARISE!

In the preceding chapters, one could be forgiven for thinking that to make a difference one needs to be involved in a big way in a defined sphere. Indeed, having critiqued the 'seven mountains of influence', I have then gone on to write about the arts, business, finance etc. Before seeking to make sure that my emphasis is clearly on 'the small people' like you and I, I will underline again that I am not suggesting that the top 3% of the mountains are our goal. Indeed given the nature of the hostility and my understanding of the mark of the beast, it is often the case that there is a strong spiritual resistance to anyone getting to that position. Of course there are always those, like Daniel, who were given favour and found themselves giving counsel to the high and mighty.[1] It is not that such an opportunity should be rejected, if it arises, but it would be wrong also to think that only at the top level can we influence the future.

Gates and intercession

At times I have used the term 'gates of influence' to describe what some have termed the mountains of influence (though I have

---

1 Another example given is that of Joseph, with a 'Joseph anointing' being attributed to certain influential business people without any critique of power, for through the guidance of Joseph the whole nation of Egypt was enslaved to Pharaoh.

deliberately never written of a 'gate of religion'). I have used the term gate as it describes a place of entry. In ancient cultures, the 'elders' sat in the gates to make decisions, and from that position, they could shape, but not simply dictate, what entered and what left the city. They were not sitting there to control people, but to look after the health of where the people lived. They were not responsible to control the environment in a way that took away personal choice but were to look after the 'soil' of society so that what grew would be healthy and to hold back unhealthy growth. Jesus said that the disciples were the 'salt of the earth', and in that culture when the salt came from the Dead Sea, it was profitably used at two levels. It contained phosphates and so was a very effective fertiliser, thus promoting growth; it was also put on the 'dung heap' thus acting as a disinfectant. Good growth promoted; disease contained.

That description so describes the calling of believers. There are influences on society that do not encourage health and well-being. Such influences need to be curtailed, and an environment that is conducive to health be nurtured. The place for influencers is important but I do not consider that we (believers) are always those who will be the direct influencers. However, through how we live, act, relate and pray, we have a responsibility to protect the environment so that the growth is healthy, and seed that is unhealthy does not prosper. I consider that a big success would be to be unknown and unrecognised but to be among the many who were effective so that what grew was good and healthy.

'Intercession' seems often to imply some great prayer activity, and I am thankful for those who work in that way, but I am seeking to interject a meaning that does not exclude that understanding but includes how we live, and where we position ourselves. I wish to include the ideas that our lives are a prayer to God, and as image-bearers, we are signposts in this world.

Symbolism in Scripture seems to be effective in two ways. It firstly acts as a sign pointing to the reality that it symbolises. My little life can be a signpost to a reality beyond my life. Hence how I respond to issues of sex, money and power is not simply a moral issue, but it points beyond my immediate world to the new creation that Jesus inaugurated. The second aspect regarding symbolism is that it draws what it is pointing to into the present reality. Perhaps nothing in the Universe on this matter of symbolism is as strong as the participation in the breaking of bread. Bread and wine. And if taken to the laboratory to examine the elements the report would come back, 'Even after prayer, still bread and wine.' Yet eat and drink of it 'unworthily', and the effects are not that of simply eating bread and drinking wine.[2] The simple symbolism has in some way drawn into the present situation the body and blood of Jesus. That is the ultimate power of symbolism.

This suggests that how I live, my small responses because of my faith in Jesus, makes a difference out of all proportion to the size of the act. For this reason, we need to be ever so open to God to prompt us to do something. Perhaps, in Scripture, the widow who put her small contribution into the Temple treasury made a much bigger contribution than she realised (Luke 21:1-4). Did her sacrifice accelerate the coming to an end of such a magnificent and impressive structure?[3]

We can be very thankful when there are believers who have a position where they can influence the future. In those situations,

---

2 I don't think it is correct to suggest that the one who eats and drinks in this way will always be the one who experiences the consequences. The effect will be manifest somewhere, in the words of Paul 'some of you are sick and have (prematurely) died'. This makes it all the more sobering. How I live will affect others.

3 In Luke's Gospel immediately following this story of the widow are the words of Jesus where he declares the Temple will be totally destroyed. The juxtaposition of the two passages surely suggest some measure of connection. The end of the previous chapter (Luke 20:47) contains a rebuke to the religious who 'devour widows' houses', and the subsequent flow of the text is strong. The widow puts in her money, into the institution that robs widows of their sustenance; Jesus looked up and 'saw' this act. The disciples lift their eyes and are impressed as they see the beauty of the Temple buildings; Jesus proclaims that not 'one stone will remain on another'. Religion devours the vulnerable; the vulnerable who seek to be righteous are honoured by God, and their small acts can become the catalyst to bring about huge change.

they face particular challenges as to how they exercise any influence they have. The powers might even make space for believers who do not understand the kenotic nature of God. As a result the church might rejoice, and yet the healthy outcome the kingdom of God should bring is set back years. In such situations, I think we might be witnessing two aspects: answered prayer and kingdom setback! So ironic as those two phrases ('answered prayer' and 'kingdom setback') should be a total oxymoron.

Following Jesus was once simple for me. Respond to Jesus as Saviour, read the Bible with a set of lenses that my tradition gave me, keep on track and make sure that I remained thankful for the ticket to heaven. Now, I realise that with a fresh prescription, the Bible ends up more wonderful, relevant and challenging than ever, that there is a path to follow, and as I long for heaven to come... I think you get the thrust.

I can only see the future that is healthy being made up of the multiplicity of the small. Not the uniformity of the big, the 'one size fits all' program - the small complemented by the richness of diversity.

Some will be positioned in a place of influence. Use it wisely, prayerfully, and in following Jesus, kenotically. Others will be marginalised, their gift not welcomed. Seek to live at peace with all, 'as far as is possible' (Rom. 12:18), and find a way of rejoicing that the one you follow was likewise marginalised.

The body of Christ is here to influence, to shape the world as is. Paul, working in specifically defined localities, used the highly politicised word, 'ekklesia', to describe the community he planted. The politicised term for those called to speak up concerning the future direction and to act in a way that helped shape their localities. We should expect that to continue, and with the incredible developments beyond localities (even now with 'virtual spaces'), we should also anticipate that there will be an even greater diversity of expression. Shapes can change, ways of doing things can develop, but faithfulness to the story has to continue.

*****

In the previous volume, I suggested that Paul carried a big vision, the 'spiritual' content of which would not have superseded the political. The message would have been understood as political for indeed it was. It was certainly more than an intellectual set of policies that could be followed as in some kind of manifesto, for it was shaped on a belief that the future had already arrived. With the resurrection of Jesus, a new world had already been brought to birth; therefore, old values were not appropriate. The ethics he proposed were based on behaviour suitable for a world different to that of the Imperial order. Rome instructed behaviour to be ordered 'because you are members of Rome'; Paul instructed believers to behave a certain way because they 'were members of each other'. Those who had received the Spirit of Jesus, and Spirit as in Person, were equipped to be the ones acting in that world. They were uniquely placed to live it out, to show and to inspire, and also to be persecuted.

In the course of the ongoing history of the world's interaction with the people of Jesus, there have been times of influence (for good and for bad), times of compromise and also of great opposition. The church has grappled with the questions raised. Questions such as, 'Is the church to be separate, somehow holy and set apart from the world?' And at times of extreme opposition, 'Is the world destined to always oppose the values of the kingdom?' And at times when the lines have been blurred, the question arises 'Is the world to embrace the values without embracing the Person of Jesus?'[4]

---

4 In the post-Christendom world of Europe it would seem we are at a time when there is a blurring of the lines. We can be threatened by that and quickly seek to draw clear lines where we make the call of who is in and who is out, or we embrace the season gladly rejoicing in the influence of Jesus' values extending beyond those who claim a personal allegiance to him. The provocation of others embracing the values but not the Person of Jesus means our witness will need to be clear and the presence of Christ with us so that we provoke a desire in others to meet this Jesus whose values are of eternal worth.

Those, and many more, questions persist. This volume has not answered them all. In this book, you will have had hints at my responses to the questions; my responses, not the final word, and my responses at this time and context. We can, and should, seek to make our response so that at this time in history, we are faithful to the trajectory as we understand it. To do that, we need wisdom from heaven, grace toward one another, and an insatiable draw to the world, the environment where God has placed us.

The future will be manifest through:

The multiplicity of the small
and the richness of diversity.

JOURNAL

- JOURNAL -

- JOURNAL -

- JOURNAL -

- JOURNAL -

- JOURNAL -

- JOURNAL -

- JOURNAL -

- JOURNAL -

- JOURNAL -

- JOURNAL -

- JOURNAL -